POTLUCK

*Exploring
North American Meals,
Culinary Practices, and Places*

*Including a Culinary Tour
of Canada and the United States*

POTLUCK

Exploring
North American Meals,
Culinary Practices, and Places

Raymond C. Clark
Jack Miller

Pro Lingua Associates

Pro Lingua Associates, Publishers
74 Cotton Mill Hill, Suite A 315
Brattleboro, Vermont 05301 USA
Office: 802-257-7779
Orders: 800-366- 4775
Email: info@ProLinguaAssociates.com
WebStore www.ProLinguaAssociates.com
SAN: 216-0579

At Pro Lingua
our objective is to foster an approach
to learning and teaching that we call
interplay, the **inter**action of language
learners and teachers with their materials,
with the language and culture,
and with each other in active, creative
and productive **play**.

The photographs used in the book are from the agency Dreamstime.com. They are as follows:

i ❧ Emanel cooking pot © Liouthe, ii ❧ © Monkey Business, iii ❧ Spanish Chicken Casserole Stew © Joseph Gough xiii ❧ Vegetables in cooking pot © Inga Nielsen, 1 ❧ Sausage and egg breakfast © Msphotographic 5 ❧ Breakfast cereal with blueberries © Msphotographic, 9 ❧ Traditional Manhattan Brunch © Olgany 13 ❧ Fifteen bean soup and sandwich © Warren Price, 17 ❧ Sandwich and fruits © Inkaphotoimage 21 ❧ Italian pizza with cherry tomatoes © Natalia Lisovshaya, 25 ❧ Boston baked beans © Timothy Grover 29 ❧ Sirloin steak © Akeeris, 33 ❧ Salmon seafood dinner © Mark Skalny 37 ❧ Multigeneration family Thanksgiving © Monkey Business Images, 41 ❧ Cookout gas grill © Ken Cole 45 ❧ Biracial family picnic © Glenda Powers, 49 ❧ Fast food hamburger meal © Joao Virissimo 53 ❧ Busy coffee shop © Monkey Business Images, 57 ❧ **a** Mexican © Josshua Rainey, **b** Thai © Tratong 57 **c** Chinese © Kornwa, **d** Japanese © Neacsu Razvan Chirnoaga, **e** Italian © Chonakan Isarankura Na Ayudhya 57 **f** French chicken in wine © Olga Krigerm, 61 ❧ Beer flight © Dreamer82, Draft at pub © Bogdan Hoda 65 ❧ Father and daughter shopping © Monkey Business Images, 69 ❧ Farmers' Market © Russ Ensley 73 ❧ Girl makes salad © Britvich, Bright kitchen © Irina88w, 77 ❧ Ice cream © John Young, Fat © Nomadsoul1 81 ❧ Halloumi/vegetable kebabs © Olgany, 85 ❧ Kitchen stove © Mitchell Barutha 89 ❧ Cookbook © Iakov Filimonov, 93 ❧ Map of North America © Dan Wallace, 97 ❧ Seafood chowder © Foodio, 98 ❧ Sloppy Joe © David Smith, Boy eating sandwich © Andre Adams 100 ❧ Eggs Benedict © Marshall Turner, Huevos Rancheros © Monkey Business Images, 192 ❧ Old Quebec City © Martial Genest, front cover ❧ Baked Beans © Timothy Grover, back cover ❧ TexMex Tacos © Marazem, Tasty, Spicy Chili Con Carne Casserole © stockcreations.

This book was set in the Century Oldstyle type face designed in 1909 by Morris Fuller Benton at the American Type Founders, based on Century Roman which was designed by his father, Linn B. Benton, for Century Magazine in 1894 and L.B.Benton's Century in 1900. These faces, noted for their strength and great legibility, have remained popular around the world, and there are many versions developed by designers for digital type. The book was printed and bound by Royal Palm Press in Punta Gorda, Florida. Designed by Arthur A. Burrows.

Printed in the United States of America
Third Edition, third printing 2019. 10,950 copies in print

Preface

This is the second edition of Potluck, originally published in 1985. It was sold until 2006, when it went out of print after selling over 10,000 copies. As each year since then has passed, I have considered a second edition, but other priorities continued to get in the way. Finally, my good friend and co-author of this edition, Jack Miller, at my request revised my original readings and added several new ones. I re-wrote the exercises, and finally we have a new edition in print.

Ray Clark
July, 2014

Acknowledgement

Thanks to Andy Burrows for suggesting the original title and offering many suggestions on the content. And thanks to Janie Duncan for her help with the first edition.

Ray Clark
Jack Miller

Contents

Introduction ❧ ix

User's Guide ❧ x

Introductory Lesson ❧ xi

1 ❧ **Breakfast: Scrambled, Over, or Sunny Side Up** ❧ 1 CD 1, tracks 1 and 2

Answers begin on page 120

sweeten	grind	prepare	fry
scramble	mix	boil	poach
beat	slice	spread	chop

2 ❧ **Breakfast Cereals, Breads, and Pastries** ❧ 5 CD 1, tracks 3 and 4

processed	crisp	flake	crunchy
fortified	coated	snack	ingredient
split	bake	powdered	granular

3 ❧ **Breakfast + Lunch = Brunch** ❧ 9 CD 1, tracks 5 and 6

occasion	socialize	appetizer	alcoholic
stir	squeezed	fancy	preserve
cure	smoked	sweet tooth	brew

4 ❧ **Lunch: Soup 'n' Sandwich** ❧ 13 CD 1, tracks 7 and 8

grilled	melt	sip	spoon
thick	stew	chunks	deli
kosher	pickle	spoil	chips

5 ❧ **The Lunch Box and Brown Bag** ❧ 17 CD 1, tracks 9 and 10

pack	container	thermos	wrap
fresh	moist	stale	can
shell	crumb	core	skin

6 ❧ **Pizza** ❧ 21 CD 1, tracks 11 and 12

dish	taste	dough	topping
oven	serve	crust	grate
mild	crumble	deliver	order

7 ❧ **Comfort Food** ❧ 25 CD 1, tracks 13 and 14

casserole	starch	carbohydrate	noodle
canned	sauce	potholder	leftover
flavor	mash	vegetarian	pudding

8 ❧ **Dinner** ❧ 29 CD 1, tracks 15 and 16

supper	dessert	rare	deep fried
course	dressing	medium	decaf
entree	well-done	peeled	doggy bag

9 ❧ Seafood Dinner ❧ 33   CD 1, tracks 17 and 18

seafood	raw	staple	fresh-caught
shellfish	cracked	fillet	freezer
batter	frozen	bones	farm-raised

10 ❧ Thanksgiving ❧ 37   CD 1, tracks 19 and 20

harvest	domestic	roast	baste
stuffing	grace	feast	carve
ladle	creamed	cultivation	mince

11 ❧ Cookouts ❧ 41   CD 1, tracks 21 and 22

grill	charcoal	dip	skewer
crush	whip	clambake	pit
barbecue	spit	tailgate	vendor

12 ❧ Picnics ❧ 45   CD 1, tracks 23 and 24

picnic basket	blanket	tablecloth	cooler
camp stove	soft drink	jug	napkin
garbage	compost	dehydrated	alfresco

13 ❧ Fast Food: For Here or to Go? ❧ 49   CD 2, tracks 1 and 2

deli	food cart	ready-made	condiments
greasy	lid	straw	unappetizing
steam	wrap	disposable	recycle

14 ❧ Coffee Shops ❧ 53   CD 2, tracks 3 and 4

gourmet	regular	caffeine	stimulant
dark roast	aroma	pastry	coffee beans
ground	mug	barista	atmosphere

15 ❧ International Restaurants ❧ 57   CD 2, tracks 5 and 6

ethnic	exotic	specialty	spicy
inviting	familiar	chopsticks	silverware
formal	reservations	customer	take out

16 ❧ Brewpubs ❧ 61   CD 2, tracks 7 and 8

tasteless	weak	brewery	on tap
draft	keg	bartender	foam
head	booth	sports bar	regulars

17 ❧ Supermarkets ❧ 65   CD 2, tracks 9 and 10

department	reusable	aisle	produce
dairy	goods	prepared foods	salad bar
checkout	cashier	scan	bar code

18 ❧ **Convenience Stores, Coops, and Farmers' Markets** ❧ 69   CD 2, tracks 11 and 12

groceries	beverages	organic	stocking
certified	supplies	free-range	local
seasonal	picker	locavore	grower

19 ❧ **The Kitchen** ❧ 73   CD 2, tracks 13 and 14

recipe	measure	cut up	equipment
tablespoon	teaspoon	bowl	knife
paring knife	spatula	gadget	appliance

20 ❧ **Health and Food** ❧ 77   CD 2, tracks 15 and 16

diet	nutrition	obese	calorie
portion	junk food	diabetes	allergic
gluten	intolerant	label	anorexic

21 ❧ **Vegetarianism** ❧ 81   CD 2, tracks 17 and 18

grains	alternative	greens	tofu
pasta	contain	stock	poultry
vegan	avoid	raw food	vitamin

22 ❧ **Cooking** ❧ 85   CD 2, tracks 19 and 20

stove	rack	broiler	burner
coil	flame	sauté	sear
evaporate	simmer	thermometer	device

23 ❧ **Recipes** ❧ 89   CD 2, tracks 21 and 22

pot	pan	step	liquid
dry	flour	quart	pint
cup	scale	thaw	rinse

24 ❧ **Summing it up: A Culinary Tour of North America** ❧ 93
   CD 2, tracks 23 and 24

Appendix One: Herbs and Spices ❧ 96

Appendix Two: Recipes ❧ 98

Appendix Three: Menus ❧ 104

Appendix Four: North American Restaurants on the Web ❧ 119

Answers ❧ 120

Food Names Index ❧ 126

Key Word Index ❧ 128

Introduction

Potluck is a photocopyable reader and vocabulary development text that focuses on the words associated with preparing, serving, and eating food in the United States and Canada. As such it also examines the role of food in North American English culture.

The text is written for the intermediate-level English language learner. Most of it is appropriate for learners from middle school to adult.

There are 24 lessons, answers to the exercises, three appendicies, and two indices. The whole book is photocopyable. Each of the lessons follows a set format of four pages. There are also two CDs for optional listening and pronunciation practice. The CDs have two tracks for each lesson. The first is simply the food names on the first page of the lesson; the second is the reading.

The opening page includes the title of the lesson and a photo to stimulate interest and discussion. The page also includes the names of foods that will be mentioned in the reading. There is an index of these food names after the appendix.

The second page is a one-page reading with key words in bold type. In most lessons the reading explores the cultural aspects of the reading's topic. The key words are also indexed.

Pages 3 and 4 are exercises that will help the learners explore the usage of the key words, sometimes in very different contexts.

The final lesson is a longer summary review with no exercises. Many of the key words are found in this summary.

The three appendices include a spice and herb chart, 6 pages of recipes, 10 menus, and a list of websites for further exploration of restaurants in the United States and Canada.

User's Guide

As a photocopyable text, Potluck can be used as the occasion demands, or as a regular part of a curriculum, perhaps one lesson per week. Although the lessons can be used in any order, it is recommended that you proceed through the lessons from first to last. This will maximize the effect of the vocabulary being recycled from one lesson to the next.

The book can be used in a variety of ways, but a suggested procedure is to begin with the brief introductory lesson that explains "potluck" and introduces the students to the format of the exercises.

The following is a suggested procedure to maximize the value of each lesson.

1. Hand out the opening page. Hold a brief discussion on the title of the lesson and the photo. Have the students talk about the topic and what it is like in their country. Then, have them talk about what they know about the topic in the United States or Canada.

2. Review the food names on the first page. You can use the CD or have the students repeat the name after you for pronunciation. Check to see which food names are new for your students. At this point you can either spend time explaining the items, and if possible bringing in the actual item, or having the students work in small groups to work on the meanings. At the end of the group sessions, you can have them use dictionaries or tell them to listen to/read the passage and see if they can get the meaning from the context in the passage. You can also do a guessing game to discover meanings. For example,

   > "Teacher, what is 'egg'?"
   > "Chickens produce me. I have a shell. You break my shell to eat me. "
   > "Ah! I know. 'Egg' in my language is X."

3. Have the learners read the passage (page 2). This can be done at home or in class. A suggested in-class procedure is to have the class read the passage orally to each other in small groups as you circulate, listening, asking, and trying to keep each group on pace so that they end their reading at more or less the same time. Encourage the readers to understand the key words from the context of the surrounding sentences. If you use the CDs, you can have the class listen to the reading first to hear the correct pronunciation of the passage. Finally, as a whole class activity, clear up any questions about the passage or the key words.

4. Hand out the exercises (pages 3 and 4) and have the learners do them. This can also be done in small groups or pairs, or as homework for individuals. If done in class, a time limit should be set. As a group finishes, check their answers or give them the answers from the back of the book. When the last group finishes, have the first group read their answers.

Using the Appendices

Spice and Herb Chart. Notice that each entry begins with a verb, and many of the entries have the same spice or herb. Give the learners the chart. Try this scanning activity. "Class, how is caraway used?" One by one, the learners read the appropriate entry.

Recipes. Bring the ingredients in and have the learners walk through putting it all together.

Menus. At an appropriate time, have the learners role play being at a restaurant and ordering a breakfast, lunch, dinner, etc.

Introductory Lesson: Potluck

"Ali, what are you doing tonight? Can you come for dinner? You'll have to take potluck, OK?"

What do you say to this **invitation**? What does it mean? What is "potluck"?

This is an **informal** invitation. It is not a planned dinner. The **host** wants you to come, but you'll have to take whatever is being prepared. As the **guest**, you're being asked to **share** what is "in the pot."

****

"Maria, we're having a potluck Saturday night. Can you come?"

How do you respond to this, and what do you do?

This is also an informal invitation to dinner, but you are expected to bring a **dish**. Often a salad or casserole, or perhaps a dessert would be expected. Sometimes the host suggests something. If not, it would be appropriate to say, "Sure! I'd love to. What can I bring?"

Sometimes the host may also say, "**BYOB.**" That means bring your own **bottle** (drinks).

Do the exercises on the next page.

Exercises

I. Match the phrase on the left with a phrase on the right to form a sentence.

1. A dinner invitation _____   A. comes to the dinner.

2. It will be informal, _____   B. to each have the same thing.

3. The host _____   C. prepares the dinner.

4. The guest _____   D. bring your own bottle (drinks).

5. To share is _____   E. can be for potluck.

6. "Dish" can mean _____   F. so wear comfortable clothing.

7. BYOB means _____   G. something to put food in
or something to eat.

II. Fill in the blank with a key word.

invitation   guest   bottle   informal
share   host   dish

1. The _____ prepares the dinner.

2. The _____ comes to the dinner.

3. They will _____ whatever the host has.

4. BYOB means bring your own _____.

5. An _____ is a request.

6. If it's _____ don't wear a suit.

7. A salad or a casserole is a _____.

Answers.

I Match: 1E, 2F, 3C, 4A, 5B, 6G, 7D

II Fill in: 1 host, 2 guest 3 share 4 bottle, 5 invitation, 6 informal, 7 dish

POTLUCK

TABLE SETTING

Breakfast: Scrambled, Over, or Sunny Side Up

coffee   milk   cream   sugar   beans   fruit

vegetable juice   tea   hot chocolate

energy drink   egg   yolk   egg whites   shell

onion   mushroom   cheese   omelet   bacon

sausage   ham   pork   toast   butter

jam   jelly   hash browns   potatoes   grits

Breakfast is the first meal of the day, and for many people breakfast begins with a cup of hot coffee. Some people drink their coffee black, and others add milk, cream, or a creamer – a non-dairy powder. Many people **sweeten** their coffee by adding sugar. For some people, making coffee is very important. They buy the best coffee beans, **grind** the beans just before pouring the water (at the perfect temperature) into the filter where the **ground** beans are. Some people choose tea or hot chocolate rather than coffee.

Another breakfast drink is fruit or vegetable juice. If you are in a big hurry and want to save time, an energy drink can substitute for breakfast.

After or with the coffee and the juice, there are eggs. The eggs can be **prepared** in different ways. **Fried** eggs are made by breaking the eggs into a hot **frying** pan. Sunny-side-up eggs are cooked without turning the eggs over, so that the yolk (the yellow center of the egg) will remain soft or runny. "Over" means that the eggs are turned and cooked on both sides. **Scrambled** eggs are prepared by **mixing** the yolks and whites together in a bowl. Then the mixture is poured into a pan and scrambled (mixed) as it is cooking. Eggs are also **boiled**. If the yolk is cooked until it is hard, the egg is called hard boiled. If the yolk is cooked for only three or four minutes, it is soft boiled, because the yolk will be soft. **Poached** eggs are also cooked in boiling water, but they are not cooked in the shell. An omelet is prepared by breaking the shell and **beating** the yolk and white into a mixture, but the mixture is not scrambled as it cooks. Onions, mushrooms, and cheese are often added to an omelet.

Bacon, sausage, or ham is often served for breakfast along with the eggs. Bacon usually comes in long, thin **slices**. Sausage comes in links which look something like hot dogs, or in patties – flat circular cakes of ground meat. Ham is served as a flat, thin slice. These breakfast meats are usually all pork, though sausage is sometimes made from other meats.

Toast is slices of bread toasted in a toaster. It is often served with bacon and eggs. The toast is usually buttered, meaning the butter is spread on the toast with a knife. Fruit jams and jellies are **spreads** that are spread on the toast.

Two other foods are sometimes served with a bacon and eggs breakfast. Hash browns are **chopped** potatoes that are lightly fried in a pan. In the southern part of the United States, grits are popular. Grits are made from ground corn and are usually served with butter. (460)

I. Match the phrase on the left with a phrase on the right to form a sentence.

1. To sweeten ____   A. is a flat, thin piece.
2. To grind something ____   B. you cut into small pieces.
3. To prepare ____   C. you mix or beat.
4. To fry ____   D. you cook it in very hot water.
5. To scramble ____   E. you crush a hard substance into a powder.
6. To boil something ____   F. you cook something in a frying pan.
7. To chop something ____   G. is cooked in water.
8. To spread jam or butter ____ H. you fix or make something.
9. A poached egg ____   I. means to add sugar.
10. A slice ____   J. you apply it to toast or bread.

II. Fill in the blank with the correct form of the word and the correct pronoun (**it** or **them**).

1. I like my coffee **sweet**. Then I'll _____ _____ for you.

2. I like my eggs **scrambled**. Then I'll _____ _____ for you.

3. I like my eggs **boiled**. Then I'll _____ _____ for you.

4. I like my eggs **fried**. Then I'll _____ _____ for you.

5. I like my toast **sliced**. Then I'll _____ _____ for you.

6. I like the whites and yolk **beaten**. Then I'll _____ _____ for you.

7. I like my ham **chopped**. Then I'll _____ _____ for you.

8. I like jam **spread** on my toast. Then I'll _____ _____ on the toast.

9. I like **poached** eggs. Then I'll _____ _____ for you.

10. I like to buy **ground** coffee. Then I don't need to _____ _____.

11. Breakfast has not been **prepared**. You're right! I'll _____ _____.

12. I need the **mixer** for this. I can _____ _____ for you.

Answers on 120

III. Fill in the blank with a form of a key word.

1. Hash brown potatoes are _____ ed by first _____ ing the potatoes into small pieces.

2. Some people like to add sugar to coffee to _____en it.

3. P_____ed eggs are cooked in _____ ing water.

4. S_____ed eggs are cooked in a _____ing pan.

5. An omelet is _____ed by first _____ ing the egg yolks and whites together into a _____ture.

6. Some people eat only buttered toast, but I like to _____ jam on it.

7. Ham, bacon, and bread can all be _____ed.

8. I like to _____ my coffee beans just before drinking.

9. Do you like your eggs _____ied, _____ed, or _____ed?

10. "Let me _____ some breakfast for you," she said.

IV. Fill in the blanks. In some cases there may be more than one possible answer.

This morning the new cook _____ breakfast for me. I asked him to fix me bacon and scrambled eggs with one _____ of toast with a fruit _____. I asked him to _____ some coffee beans and _____ my coffee with one spoon of sugar. So what do I get? A strange _____ of bacon and eggs. The bacon was _____ into little pieces, and _____ with the eggs. The bread was _____ into little strips. This _____ was _____ on the toast. On the side were coffee beans covered in sugar. I asked him what he had done, and he said, "You asked me to mix you some bacon and eggs on _____ toast and _____ the beans."

Breakfast Cereals, Breads, and Pastries

cereal	bread	pastry	grain	wheat	oats
corn	rice	milk	honey	raisins	oatmeal
granola	flour	fat	shortening	muffin	
bagels	cream cheese		donuts (doughnuts)		
cream	sweet rolls	cinnamon			
nuts	scones	croissants			

Many people, especially children, like cereals for breakfast. Cereals are made from grains such as wheat, oats, corn, and rice. Some cereals are eaten hot and some are cold.

Hot cereals are cooked with water or milk to form a soft food that is eaten with a spoon. Milk and sweeteners such as sugar, honey, or raisins are added to the cereal. Oatmeal is one of the most popular hot cereals.

Cold cereals are made from grains that have been **processed** into **crisp** pieces that come in many sizes and shapes. The most common shape, called a **flake**, is very thin and **crunchy** – it breaks easily and with a noise (a **crunch**). Cold cereals are known by their trade names, and the variety seems endless. Some of the better known are Corn Flakes, Wheaties, Rice Krispies, Shredded Wheat, Cheerios, and Captain Crunch. Many cold cereals have been **fortified** with vitamins to make the cereal more **nutritious**. Some are **coated** with sugar. A popular mostly unprocessed cold cereal is granola, which is also eaten dry as a **snack**.

The basic **ingredient** of breads and pastries is flour. Pastries are made with a special fat called shortening to make the pastry light and flaky, or butter if the bakery wants a somewhat higher quality. Here are some common types of breakfast breads and pastries:

Muffins — small, round cakes that look like they were **baked** in a cup.

English muffins — a round bread that is split down the middle with a knife or fork and toasted.

Bagels — a round bread with a hole in the middle. Bagels are boiled and then baked. They are split in half and often eaten with a smooth white cheese spread called cream cheese.

Donuts (sometimes spelled *doughnuts*) — deep fried sweet cakes that are round. Typically, they have a hole in the middle, but sometimes there are jams, jellies or cream in the middle. Powdered sugar is frequently applied to the outside.

Sweet rolls (some kinds are called *Danish*) — a sweet, sticky pastry with cinnamon, nuts, raisins, or fruit-filled centers.

Scones and *croissants* — rich pastries that provide a nice contrast with the taste of coffee. (357)

I. Match the phrase on the left with a phrase on the right to form a sentence.

1. Processed food is _____   A. high in food value.
2. Something that is crisp _____   B. what is in the food.
3. A flake is _____   C. a small, thin piece of something.
4. Crunchy foods _____   D. modified by a procedure.
5. Fortified food is _____   E. food that is eaten between meals.
6. Nutritious food is _____   F. is cut into two pieces.
7. To coat is _____   G. make a sound when chewed.
8. Ingredients are _____   H. to cover with something.
9. If it is baked, _____   I. covered with a very fine coat.
10. Something that is split _____ J. made stronger or more nutritious.
11. A snack is _____   K. it is cooked in an oven.
12. Powdered means _____   L. is not soft.

II. Fill in the blank with the correct form of the word.

ingredients	nutrition	powdered	process	flake	coat
crunchy	snack	baked	split	crisp	fortify

1. The _____ takes a long time.

2. A snow_____ can have a beautiful design.

3. We need to put on a second _____ of paint.

4. In the fall we _____ a lot of wood for the stove.

5. The science of _____ is of great interest to me.

6. I like my potatoes _____.

7. Potato chips are a popular _____ .

8. All the _____ in this bread are natural.

9. The evening air was cool and _____.

10. I like nuts because they are very _____.

11. To _____ is to make stronger.

12. _____ milk will last a long time.

Answers on 120

III. Fill in the blank with a form of a key word.

1. I like wheat _____ more than corn _____.

2. Sugar is an _____ in this cereal.

3. Sugar-_____ cereals are not good for us.

4. He loves to spend time _____ bread.

5. I'm hungry and I can't wait for dinner. Let's have a _____.

6. The _____ of applying for a permit takes a long time.

7. Many years ago, people built _____ in this spot for defense against their enemies.

8. The _____ information is on the side of the package.

9. These flakes have lost their _____ness. They are no longer _____.

10. My friend makes a delicious _____ pea soup.

11. It's called The _____ House because it's where they kept their gun _____.

IV. Fill in the blank with a form of a key word.

Yesterday it snowed. Great big beautiful _____ floated down and covered

the ground in a soft, white _____. The trees looked sugar-_____!

Good enough to eat, but of course not very _____. But then the

_____, cold air warmed up, and suddenly the ground was covered with frozen

snow. It _____ when you walked on it.

Inside it smelled so nice. Mom had _____ some great cookies with all natural

_____. No _____ food in our house! They were

delicious! They were sweet and _____ like the snow.

Dad was outside _____ wood for the fireplace. Mom had fixed a light

_____ that was waiting for Dad to come in and be _____ with a

tall mug of hot chocolate.

Breakfast + Lunch = Brunch

chips shrimp dip tomato vodka celery

orange grapefruit eggs Benedict

hollandaise sauce lemon huevos rancheros

corned beef hash lox corn cobs challah

pancakes waffles French toast maple syrup

Sunday morning is a good time to sleep longer than usual and then have a late breakfast or early lunch: the brunch. Although breakfast at home is not usually a social affair, brunch often is. It is not uncommon to invite friends to share brunch or meet them at a restaurant. It's a good **occasion** for **socializing** and forgetting about the cares of daily life for a while.

The brunch table often includes an **appetizer,** such as shrimp with a dip, and brunch is sometimes served with a Bloody Mary – a popular morning **alcoholic** drink. It is a mixed drink of tomato juice and vodka. A celery stick is often used as a **stirrer** for stirring the drink. Other people prefer freshly-**squeezed** orange or grapefruit juice.

Eggs are commonly served for brunch, but they are often a bit **fancier** than the usual scrambled or fried. Omelets are popular. Eggs Benedict is another favorite; it is a poached egg and a slice of ham or Canadian bacon on an English muffin half, topped with hollandaise sauce (butter, egg yolk, pepper, and lemon). Huevos rancheros from Mexico is another favorite egg dish, and still another is poached eggs on corned beef hash. In this case, "corn" has nothing to do with the vegetable corn; it refers to a method of **preserving** the meat by **curing** it with salt.

A favorite bakery item for brunch is a bagel spread with cream cheese and lox (**smoked** salmon). In fact, many kinds of meat (bacon and ham, for example) besides salmon are cured by smoking – hanging the meat in air inside a smokehouse. Hickory wood or corn cobs are burned to produce a pleasant smoky flavor in the meat. At a brunch you can also find scones and fancy toast such as cinnamon-raisin or challah (egg bread). These are all served with plenty of jam, cream cheese, or butter.

In the winter, a lot of people prefer hot dishes such as pancakes, waffles, or French toast, topped with butter and a syrup. Maple syrup is a special favorite. People with a **sweet tooth** like lots of it. And nearly everyone has coffee at a brunch. It's usually **brewed** from freshly ground coffee beans from Colombia, Brazil, Ethiopia, or some other distant land.

When brunch is over and the dirty dishes have been cleared away, the table wiped, the dishes washed and put away, people like to settle down with another cup of coffee and the Sunday newspaper, sitting out on the deck in the summer. The eating and socializing have been so relaxing and enjoyable that people don't want it to end. (438)

I. Match the phrase on the left with a phrase on the right to form a complete sentence.

1. An occasion is _____   A. is liking sweet things.
2. Socializing is _____   B. a stick used for mixing a drink.
3. An appetizer is _____   C. is cured in a smokehouse.
4. An alcoholic drink _____   D. making a drink such as coffee or beer.
5. A stirrer is _____   E. a time or event.
6. Freshly-squeezed _____   F. is attractive, and not usually simple.
7. Something that is fancy _____   G. enjoying the company of others.
8. To preserve is _____   H. something eaten before the meal.
9. Curing is the process of _____   I. is a drink like wine or beer.
10. Smoked meat _____   J. means something is crushed for the juice.
11. Having a sweet tooth _____   K. saving something so it will last longer.
12. Brewing is _____   L. preserving a meat with salt.

II. Fill in the blanks with a form of a key word.

occasionally   fancy   alcohol   smoking   socialize   stir
preserving   sweet tooth   appetizer   squeeze   curing   brew

1. There is _____ in a Bloody Mary.

2. A celery stick can be used to _____ the drink.

3. We have brunch _____ – maybe once a month.

4. _____ and _____ are two ways of _____ meats.

5. For brunch today, nothing _____, just bacon and eggs.

6. After you _____ the oranges, will you _____ the coffee?

7. My _____ is making me use too much syrup.

8. To begin, let's have smoked salmon as an _____ .

9. Brunch is a great way to _____ with the neighbors.

Answers on 120

III. Fill in the blanks with a form of a key word.

1. I need a _____ for my coffee.
2. I bought some _____ ham for your sandwiches.
3. Let's not use our _____ tablecloth.
4. _____ coffee is much tastier than instant coffee.
5. I don't have a _____ . I never eat dessert.
6. Billy, don't _____ the cat. You'll hurt it.
7. I'm not hungry; I'll just have an _____ .
8. She's very quiet and not good at _____.
9. Why are you wearing a jacket and tie? What's the _____ ?
10. Is there any _____ in this drink?
11. My mother used to _____ tomatoes in glass jars.
12. There is no _____ for some diseases.

IV. Use one of the key words in each of these blanks.

> Hi, Janie. What are you up to this morning? . . . Uh, huh, then why not do a
>
> little _____. Come over for brunch. . . . Yeah, the whole works –
>
> our _____ tablecloth, some great _____ bacon that was
>
> _____ at the Northside Smoke House. . . .
>
> No, no need to bring anything unless you want something_____ to
>
> drink. . . . No, we're just having coffee. And we have celery if you want some
>
> _____ . I'm opening a jar of Aunt Millie's pickles – all-natural,
>
> no _____. Bob's _____ some Costa Rican Arabica,
>
> and _____ some organic Chilean oranges; they're really
>
> _____ . . . No, It's not a special _____ . . . . Sure, bring an
>
> _____ . Lox would be great. . . . OK, see you at 11:00 ?

Lunch: Soup 'n' Sandwich

cheese   tomato   tuna fish   chowder

milk   potatoes   mushroom   clam   oyster

beef   carrots   peas   crackers   rolls

lettuce   salad   vinegar   mayonnaise

Both at home and in restaurants, soup and sandwich is a popular easy-to-fix lunch. One popular combination is a **grilled** cheese sandwich and tomato soup. The sandwich is made by putting slices of cheese between two slices of bread. It is cooked on a hot, flat surface that has been lightly coated with oil or butter. The sandwich is grilled on both sides until the cheese becomes hot and soft, and **melts**. A sandwich called a melt has only one slice of bread. It has ingredients such as tuna fish placed on top of the bread and then covered with cheese. Then the whole thing is **toasted** until the cheese melts.

Soup is served in a cup or bowl. Because it is hot, it is **sipped** carefully from the cup or **spooned** from the bowl with a soup spoon. Chowders are soups that are made with milk and potatoes. Fish and clam chowder are especially well known. Milk is also an ingredient in various soups that are called cream soups, such as cream of tomato and mushroom. Oyster stew is a kind of **thick** chowder made with oysters. Everything is **stewed** slowly for a long time. Stews are very similar to soups, but they are always thicker: that is, they contain more solid ingredients. Another favorite stew is beef stew, made with **chunks** of beef and potatoes, slices of carrot, peas, and pieces of onion. A bowl of soup is often served with crackers, a dry, thin and crisp bakery product that comes in a variety of shapes, sizes, and flavors.

Sandwiches are made with almost every kind of bread. In addition to sliced bread, they are made with rolls. Long, round rolls are sliced lengthwise and used for making subs, short for submarines. A chain has popularized the name sub and offers foot-long sandwiches. They are also known as grinders, heroes, hoagies, poor boys, Italian sandwiches and by many other names. These sandwiches contain meat, lettuce, cheese, and almost anything else people want in them.

Many people go to the **deli** (delicatessen) for their sandwiches. The deli specializes in ready-to-eat foods, especially cold sliced meats (called cold cuts), cheeses, and salads. Some delis specialize in Jewish food that is **kosher**, or properly prepared according to Jewish religious customs. "Kosher" can also have a general meaning of "proper."

Pickles are commonly served with sandwiches. The verb to pickle refers to the practice of keeping food in a special liquid of salt and vinegar so it will not **spoil**. Potato or corn **chips** are often eaten with sandwiches. Chips are thin slices that have been deep-fried or baked. An alternative to potato chips is potato salad, small chunks of potato mixed with hard-boiled eggs, mayonnaise, and celery. A lot of delis now have a salad bar where you can pick whatever salads you want from a large selection of items. (479)

I. Match the phrase on the left with a phrase on the right to form a sentence.

1. A grilled sandwich is cooked _____   A. food in that deli?
2. She toasted the tuna fish sandwich _____   B. very slowly.
3. Has the cheese _____   C. the soup into a bowl.
4. Chowders are _____   D. stew for lunch.
5. The waiter spooned _____   E. on a hot, flat surface.
6. My father often has oyster _____   F. in the toaster oven.
7. Cut the potatoes _____   G. melted yet?
8. Do they have kosher _____   H. thicker than soup.
9. This food is spoiled; _____   I. with a pickle and chips.
10. The sandwich special comes _____   J. into small chunks.
11. He sipped the hot soup _____   K. I can't eat it.

II. Fill in the blanks with a form of a key word.

grilled	chips	stews	spoons	toasted	pickle
chunks	melted	thick	sip	kosher	spoiled

1. I'll have a _____ cheese sandwich.

2. Do you want it _____ or grilled?

3. Those slices of bread are too _____. They need to be thinner.

4. It's hot. _____ it slowly.

5. There aren't many _____ of beef in it.

6. _____ are cooked slowly for at least an hour.

7. We don't have any soup _____. Use the tea spoons.

8. It comes with potato _____ and a _____.

9. What she did wasn't very _____ .

10. Her rude comments _____ a wonderful dinner.

11. My ice has _____. May I have some more?

Answers on 120

III. Fill in the blanks with a form of a key word.

1. We're all out of clam chowder. Then I'll have oyster _____.
2. The soup is very hot. Then I'll _____ it slowly.
3. We're all out of potato salad. Then I'll have potato _____.
4. We're all out of tuna. Then I'll have a _____ cheese.
5. That's not right. It just isn't _____.
6. Cook it until it _____ , and it's hard to stir.
7. These pieces of meat are big. Then I'll cut them into _____.
8. I don't want it fried or grilled. Then I'll _____ it.
9. I dropped my _____ on the floor. I'll get another for you.
10. This tastes awful. It must be _____.
11. The cheese isn't _____. Then the oven must be off.
12. I picked a lot of cucumbers. Then I'll _____ some.

IV. Fill in the blanks with a form of one of the key words.

Professor Cook's Word Study for Today

Today you were introduced to 12 words. Do you realize that all but one can be used as verbs? Well, they can. But first, which one cannot be a verb? If you said _____, you're right. So let's run down the list.

• A sandwich can be _____, or _____, and cheese can be _____.

• Hot soup can be carefully _____ and _____ into a bowl with a soup spoon.

• To make a stew thicker, it can be _____. And you can _____ vegetables like tomatoes for a long time to make them soft and mushy.

• One way of preserving food is to _____ it.

• To make something smaller you can _____ away at it.

• A large piece of something can be _____. If you do that to meat, it can _____ faster.

The Lunch Box and Brown Bag

tortilla   peanut butter   baloney

chicken   turkey   yogurt

chocolate chip   cookie

Many people, especially working people and school children, fix their lunches at home, **pack** them in a metal **container** called a lunch box, and carry them to work or school. Some people bring their lunches in a paper bag. Because paper bags are typically brown, this kind of lunch is called a "brown bag." Some bags are **thermos** lunch bags, especially made to keep hot food and drinks hot and cold food and drinks cold, for a while.

A sandwich is the principal part of a lunch box meal. A sandwich is two slices of bread with something between the two slices. **Wraps** are now very popular. They are made with a flatbread or tortilla. The ingredients are placed on the bread and then it is rolled up. Finally, the sandwich or the wrap is wrapped in plastic wrap or a small plastic bag to keep it **fresh**; otherwise, it would lose its **moistness** and become dry and **stale**.

A peanut butter sandwich is a favorite among children. Peanut butter is a thick spread made from peanuts. Many children (or the children's parents) also apply jam or jelly to their peanut butter sandwich, usually called a peanut butter and jelly sandwich. Children often call it just a "P B and J."

Another common sandwich is tuna fish, which is made by mixing **canned** tuna from a small metal container, called a can, with mayonnaise – a white spread made with egg yolk, oil, lemon, and spices.

Other common sandwiches are baloney (slices of a thick sausage called Bologna sausage, named for a city in Italy), sliced ham and cheese, and chicken or turkey. Egg, chicken, turkey, and ham are also chopped into small pieces and mixed with mayonnaise to make egg, chicken, turkey, or ham salad sandwiches. In fact, the variety of things that can be put into a sandwich is limited only by your imagination.

A hard-boiled egg, still in its **shell,** and carrot or celery sticks are also commonly found in a home-**packed** lunch. Many brown-baggers like to bring a small container of yogurt, and in winter a **thermos** that contains a hot drink. A good thermos can keep the breakfast coffee hot until lunch time.

Along with a sandwich, there is often a piece of fruit and a cookie, a small sweet cake, usually flat and round. A favorite cookie is the chocolate chip cookie that contains small pieces of chocolate. Three other popular types of cookies are **oatmeal**, **raisin**, and peanut butter. Cookie lovers might want cookies that combine two or three of those ingredients.

At the end of the day, the lunch box is carried home with only empty wrappers, bread **crumbs**, egg shells, and apple **cores** or banana **skins** inside. (455)

I. Match the phrase on the left with a phrase on the right to form a sentence.

1. To pack is _____	A. not dry.
2. A container can be _____	B. outer part of an egg.
3. A thermos is _____	C. to cover with paper, plastic, or flat bread.
4. To wrap means _____	D. to put in and seal in a can.
5. Fresh is_____	E. very small pieces of bread.
6. Moist means _____	F. its skin.
7. To can is _____	G. the inner part of an apple.
8. The shell is the _____	H. to put something in a container.
9. Crumbs are _____	I. the opposite of stale.
10. The core is _____	J. a container that keeps food cool or hot.
11. The covering of a banana is _____	K. a box.

II. Fill in the blanks with a form of a key word.

canned   thermos   wrapped   packed   moistness
contains   core   crumbs   skin
fresh/canned   shell   stale

1. Who _____ your lunch?

2. My lunch box _____ only a sandwich and an apple.

3. I slipped on a banana _____.

4. After lunch the table was covered with _____ .

5. The sandwiches are _____ in plastic.

6. _____ fruit is much better than _____ fruit.

7. There are pieces of egg _____ in my egg salad.

8. My turkey wrap has lost its _____; it's all dried out and the

   bread is _____ .

9. That apple was great; I even ate almost all the _____.

10. There's hot coffee in your _____ bottle.

Answers on 121

III. Fill in the blanks with a form of a key word.

1. A bottle is a _____, but six bottles of beer is a six- _____.
2. To cover something with paper or plastic is to _____ it, and the covering is called a _____.
3. A small, round metal container is a _____ and what is inside is _____.
4. The outside of an egg is a _____ . We need to _____ eggs carefully so the _____ doesn't crack.
5. The inside part of an apple that is not eaten is the _____. And when the _____ is removed, the apple has been _____ed.
6. The opposite condition of dryness is _____, and the opposite condition of stale is _____ .
7. After eating cookies, there are _____. And after eating an apple there is a _____ .
8. _____ bread is hard and dry, and dry _____ is itchy.

IV. Complete the conversation.

Edna: What will I _____ for your lunch today?

Ed: Oh, I'll have a turkey and cheese _____, a hard-boiled_____ , some chocolate _____ cookies, and a _____, crisp McIntosh apple.

Edna: The bread isn't very _____. You forgot to _____ it last night after dinner. And the raisin bread is _____.

Ed: Oh, well. Skip the bread.

Edna: Shall I take the _____ off the egg?

Ed: No, leave it on; otherwise it will lose its _____.

Edna: You know, we haven't any _____ fruit, but I've got a _____ of peaches.

Ed: What happened to all the fresh fruit?

Edna: The kids ate the apples. Nothing left but _____.

Ed: Bananas?

Edna: Nothing left but _____.

Ed: Cookies?

Edna: Nothing left but _____.

Ed: Oh well, I'd rather eat at the coop anyway.

Pizza

pie   bun   basil   mozzarella   Parmesan
pepperoni   goat cheese   artichoke   pineapple
soft drink   beer   wine   dessert   focaccia
olive oil   rosemary   herb

❧   21

A simple **dish** made for centuries by farmers and working people in southern Italy has conquered the world. Because it is so simple, it can be made in many ways, and it can be changed to suit many **tastes**. In Italian, the word means "pie" or "bun." But most of us know it as pizza.

Pizza is usually round but sometimes rectangular. It is made from wheat **dough** and some kind of **topping**. That's all. It is baked in a very hot **oven** for ten or fifteen minutes, taken out, cut into rectangular or triangular slices, and **served** with a salad and a drink.

The dough (or **crust**) may be thin (as in Naples, Italy) or thick (as in Chicago). The pizza can be small (for one person) or large (for three or four people). Naturally, different pizza restaurants (they are often called pizza places) claim to have the best crust. There is a lot of competition and every pizza lover has a local favorite.

People may argue about the best crust, but it is still basically something to put toppings on. The three most common toppings are tomato sauce, **grated** cheese, and basil. A margherita pizza consists of those three. But what kind of cheese? Usually, it's mozzarella, a soft, rubbery, **mild** cheese that is hard to pull apart. A lot of pizzas also contain Parmesan, a very hard, dry cheese, the opposite of mozzarella, that is grated on top of all the other ingredients.

Meat is another common topping, with sliced pepperoni, a kind of very hard sausage, most popular. Some people like soft pieces of sausage **crumbled** on their pizza. Goat cheese (soft and white), peppers, and onions are common too, but every pizza place has its specialties, which may include ham, artichokes, and even pineapple. The sky's the limit.

More than any other kind of restaurant, pizza places **deliver** to your house. You can call up your favorite place or go online to its website, **order** exactly what you want, and in about a half-hour the food will be at your front door. The delivery person drives a car with the name of the pizza place in big letters on top. You can watch for the car from your window and tell everyone "Pizza's here!" The pizza will be in a special flat box that keeps it nice and hot.

Pizza restaurants serve more than just pizza. Soft drinks, beer, wine, salads, and desserts can be found. Another popular item is a variation on pizza – focaccia. It is flat dough like a pizza but with very few toppings – usually just olive oil, salt, and rosemary, a Mediterranean herb.

In almost any city in the world these days, you can find a pizza, so you never have to be far from one. Wherever you are, it is always there as a good, simple choice for lunch or dinner. (481)

I. Match the phrase on the left with a phrase on the right to form a sentence.

1. A simple dish _____
2. Taste can mean _____
3. Dough is _____
4. A topping could be _____
5. An oven is _____
6. "Dinner is served" _____
7. The crust _____
8. Grated cheese
9. Mild can mean _____
10. To crumble means _____
11 To deliver means _____
12. To order means _____

A. tomato sauce.
B. is scraped to make small pieces.
C. to bring something to a place.
D. to request or ask for something.
E. to break into small pieces.
F. is easy to make.
G. the place where pizzas are baked.
H. a person's preferences for food.
I. not strong or hot.
J. is dough that has been cooked.
K. means the food is on the table.
L. wheat flour that has been made into a soft substance which will be baked or boiled.

II. Fill in the blanks with a form of a key word.

**milder   dishes   grate   dough   delivery   toppings
server   oven   ordered   crumble   tastes   crust**

1. Is mozzarella _____ er than Parmesan?

2. I'm hungry; where is the _____ery person?

3. We _____ ed over half an hour ago.

4. I love pizza; it's one of my favorite _____es.

5. Which _____ s do we want on our pizza?

6. Let's _____ some sausage on the pizza.

7. Don't forget to _____ the cheese.

8. In a restaurant, the waitperson is also called the _____.

9. This sauce _____s a little strange. Is it OK?

10. _____ is made with flour and water.

11. Don't put it in the _____ now; it's not hot enough.

12. I think this _____ is really too thick.

Answers on 121

❧ 23

III. Fill in the blanks with one of the key words.

1. The _____ on this pizza is quite thin.

2. Please do not _____ my pizza before six o'clock.

3. It's $14.95, and the price includes three _____.

4. I'm sorry. I didn't _____ these bread sticks.

5. I'd like some more water. Where is our _____ ?

6. This weekend, I'm going to clean the _____ .

7. _____ can mean a kind of meal or a plate.

8. Tonight's special is a _____ of the Mediterranean.

9. The weather recently has been quite _____, neither hot nor cold.

10. The cake looked good, but it _____ when I tried to eat it.

11. _____ cheese should be kept in the refrigerator.

12. Did you know that _____ can also mean "money"?

IV . Fill in the blanks with a form of one of the key words.

A: What will we have for dinner tonight?

B: How about pizza?

A: Do we have any grated _____ or other _____?

B: We don't have Parmesan, but we have some _____ cheddar.

    And we have plenty of flour, so I'll make the _____ .

A: Can you make a thin _____?

B: Sure. Or a deep _____ if you want.

A: I can _____ it already.

B: I'll get a frying pan and heat up some sausage and _____ it.

A: Uh oh!

B: What's up?

A: The _____ isn't working, remember?

B: Well, give me the phone and I'll _____ from Napoli's.

A: Do they have a _____ _____?

B: Uh …. OK, give me the car keys. I'll go.

Comfort Food

potatoes   peas   corn   rice   sugar

tuna   milk   butter   eggs   mushrooms

onions   pasta   spaghetti   chicken   ham

beef   beans   pork   brown sugar

molasses   mustard   lamb   lasagna

macaroni   cheese   meatloaf

Comfort food is seldom exciting. It is seldom new or unusual. It is seldom colorful, and it does not make you dream of foreign lands. There is a lot that it does not do, but it does very well what it is supposed to do – it makes a lot of people feel comfortable. For many, comfort food is the kind of thing mom or grandma made.

The word **"casserole"** has two meanings: it is a dish that food is cooked (usually baked) in, and it is the food itself. The dish usually contains a mixture of some meat, vegetables, and some kind of **starchy** food such as potatoes, corn, and rice. Starch, like sugar, contains **carbohydrates**, a chemical in food that the body needs.

A typical casserole is tuna-**noodle**. It couldn't be easier to make. It uses **canned** tuna, noodles, a simple white **sauce**, made with milk, butter, flour, and a couple of spices, along with eggs, mushrooms, onions, and butter. Even the busiest people can put it together and toss it into the oven for a half hour. And be careful to use **potholders** when you take it out. Noodles, by the way, are a kind of pasta, like spaghetti. Chicken can be substituted for the tuna, and you can guess the result: chicken-noodle casserole, or ham or beef. So this casserole is a good way to use **leftovers** that are in the refrigerator.

Some casseroles use only a small amount of meat, so they are especially economical. Boston baked beans is one of these. It uses just a little pork for **flavor**, as well as brown sugar, molasses, and mustard. It is often served with a sweet brown bread. Another is shepherd's pie, which, though it includes some lamb, has **mashed** potatoes as the main ingredient. Still another is lasagna, a popular Italian-style casserole. The big noodles and the tomato sauce are more important than the ground beef in lasagna.

Some casseroles use no meat at all. They are **vegetarian**. Maybe the most popular of these is macaroni and cheese, something children have pleaded for since the dish was invented. A white sauce including cheese is mixed with cooked macaroni (sometimes called elbow macaroni) and baked, like all casseroles. By the way, adults love it, too.

Almost anything can be featured in a casserole. Moussaka is Greek style and contains a lot of eggplant. Rice is the main ingredient in Turkish pilaf. Rice is also used to make rice **pudding,** a dessert. But not every comfort food is a casserole. Some are just familiar combinations like meatloaf with mashed potatoes and carrots. For most people, most of the time, the phrase comfort food makes them think of one thing – a familiar casserole. (454)

I. Match the phrase on the left with a phrase on the right to form a sentence.

1. Casseroles are _____   A. leftover.
2. Starch is _____   B. of ice cream.
3. Noodles are _____   C. to hold hot pots.
4. Canned tuna is _____   D. baked.
5. A sauce is _____   E. a dessert.
6. Use potholders _____   F. potatoes?
7. Let's eat this again as a _____ G. do not eat meat.
8. There are many flavors _____   H. not fresh.
9. Do you want fried or mashed ____ I. an ingredient in a casserole
10. Rice pudding is _____   J. a type of carbohydrate.
11. Vegetarians _____   K. a type of pasta.

II. Use the key words in the sentences below

**casserole   starch   carbohydrates   noodle   canned
sauce   potholder   pudding   leftovers   flavoring
masher   vegetarian**

1. I love chocolate _____ .

2. Let's add a little _____ to give it more taste.

3. Sugar, _____, and fibers are _____ .

4. My favorite _____ is tuna- _____ .

5. Why eat _____ vegetables, when you can get them fresh?

6. We had lots of _____ – enough for lunch tomorrow.

7. My son is a _____, and I think I should be.

8. Where's the potato _____ ?

9. Who spilled the _____ on the _____ ?

Answers on 121

III. Fill in the blank with the appropriate form of the word.

1. _____ do not eat meat.

2. I bought a _____ of tuna.

3. Will you _____ the potatoes for me?

4. _____ are a necessary part of our diet.

5. _____ are my favorite kind of pasta.

6. I don't often eat _____ for dessert.

7. We use tomato _____ when we make a pizza.

8. We ate everything; there were no _____ .

9. Toothpaste comes in many different _____ .

10. _____ are baked in an oven.

11. Potatoes are a vegetable that has a lot of _____ .

12. If you do a lot of baking, you will need good _____ .

IV. Complete the conversation.

Ed: So is everything ready for the guests?

Edna: The tuna- _____ _____is done and waiting in the oven. The

white _____ is on the table. The potatoes are _____ . And the rice

_____ is in the fridge. By the way, I added some vanilla for _____ .

Ed: Sounds good, but a little heavy on the _____, isn't it?

Edna: A little _____ never hurt anyone.

Ed: Maybe not, but Chuck is a diabetic _____ .

Edna: I know, so I made a small dish of macaroni and cheese for him.

Ed: Macaroni and cheese?

Edna: Ed, stop worrying. There won't be any _____ – nothing to throw

in the garbage _____.

Ed: There's the doorbell. Get your _____ ready!

Dinner

poultry   chicken   turkey   beef   pork   lamb

chops   ribs   roast beef   steak   lettuce

green peppers   onions   radishes   mushrooms

arugula   tomatoes   sprouts   olive oil

vinegar   potatoes   home fries

fruit   coffee   liqueur   berries   nuts

The evening meal – usually called dinner, but sometimes called **supper** – is the biggest meal of the day. In a formal meal, or at a restaurant, there may be several **courses**. Many people like to begin with an alcoholic drink. Then comes the first course, an appetizer, which may be one of many small dishes or a soup. Next, there is a salad. Then comes the main course (sometimes called an **entrée**) and, finally, something sweet, the **dessert**. The main course is often a meat. The principal kinds of meat eaten by Americans and Canadians are poultry (chicken and turkey), beef, pork, and lamb. Chicken and turkey are the most popular. For those who like chicken, some prefer the light meat (breast) and some prefer the dark meat (wings, legs, and thighs). Among the various cuts of beef (ribs, roasts, and steaks), most people's favorite is a steak. The popular cuts of pork and lamb are chops, ribs, and roasts.

The main ingredient of most salads is some type of lettuce. Green peppers, onions, radishes, mushrooms, arugula, tomatoes, and sprouts are other common ingredients. A salad **dressing** is mixed with the salad. There are many kinds of dressing: olive oil and vinegar, Italian, French, Russian, Thousand Island, and blue cheese, to name a few.

The main course in the typical steak dinner consists of steak, potatoes, and another vegetable. Some people like their steak cooked thoroughly, or **well-done**, and some people like to have it just slightly cooked, or **rare**. Somewhere between well done and rare is **medium**. A typical question at a restaurant is, "How do you want your steak?"

There is also a choice of different types of potatoes: baked, mashed, French fries, or home fries. Baked potatoes are baked in the oven in their skins. Mashed potatoes are first **peeled** – the skin is taken off – and then boiled. Then they are mashed, and some milk, butter, and salt are added. French fries are potatoes cut into strips and **deep fried**. And home fries are slices or small chunks of potatoes fried in a pan.

Finally, there is dessert. There are many kinds of desserts, but two favorites are apple pie and ice cream. Sometimes it is too difficult to decide on one or the other, so the ice cream is served on top of the pie, as pie á la mode. Today many people, thinking about their weight, prefer a more modest dessert like frozen yogurt or fruit.

The evening meal often ends with a cup of coffee – regular or **decaf** (decaffeinated) for those who are kept awake at night by caffeine. At most restaurants, it is acceptable to take home food that has not been eaten. The server can bring you a "**doggy bag**," which is really a paper box for your leftovers. (466)

I. Match the phrase on the left with a phrase on the right to form a sentence.

1. Supper is _____	A. is neither rare nor well done.
2. Dinner is served _____	B. of salad dressings.
3. French fries _____	C. you remove the skin.
4. The last course is _____	D. a decaf, please.
5. The main course _____	E. is not cooked very long.
6. There are many kinds_____	F. an evening meal.
7. A rare steak _____	G. in three courses.
8. A well-done steak _____	H. for a doggy bag.
9. A medium steak _____	I. is cooked longer than a medium.
10. To peel a potato _____	J. the dessert.
11. I'll have _____	K. is called the entrée.
12. Let's ask the server _____	L. are deep fried in a basket.

II. Fill in the blanks with a form of a key word.

supper   dessert   rare   deep fried   course   dressing
medium   decaf   entrée   well-done   peel   doggy bag

1. I want my steak _____ _____.

2. I want mine to be _____ . The inside should be quite red.

3. _____ - well means not too well done, and not really _____, either.

4. I ate only half my steak; I need a _____ .

5. I'll have the oil and vinegar _____ .

6. At our house _____ is usually at six o'clock.

7. When I make home fries, I don't _____ them.

8. Do you have _____ coffee?

9. To _____ something you need a large pot.

10. Supper may not have three _____, and it is very often just a casserole.

    We don't call the casserole an _____, and sometimes there is no appetizer

    or _____ .

Answers on 121

III. Fill on the blanks with a form of a key word.

1. I'm sorry. This isn't _____-_____ . Please cook it some more.

2. And mine is definitely not _____. Please cook it some more.

3. This one is not _____ . It is medium.

4. For _____ this evening, something quick and easy? A can of baked beans?

5. We had a full-_____ dinner at the Inn last night. We had soup as an appetizer, the _____ was a delicious steak, and the _____ was very nice tapioca pudding.

6. I ate everything; no need for a _____ .

7. The house _____ for our salad was an olive oil and vinegar.

8. We don't have French fries because our _____ isn't working.

9. This is going to be expensive. If we can't pay we may have to _____ potatoes.

IV. Fill in the blanks with a form of a key word.

Ed: Charles and Mary should be coming soon.

Edna: Everything's ready. Potatoes are _____ and mashed, the appetizers are on the table with the salad _____ . Two pies for _____ .

Ed: They were expecting a simple _____, but it will be a three-_____ dinner.

Edna: Mais oui! And the _____ will be the Jolly Butcher's best steak. And nothing is _____. That will make Mary happy; you know how she dislikes fried food.

Ed: And Mary likes her steak _____-_____, Charles is the opposite, very _____, and ours of course is neither _____ nor well-done, a perfect _____.

Edna: Remember, Ed, Charles may ask for a _____. He always does.

Seafood Dinner

fish   clams   oysters   scallops   flour

milk   eggs   crabs   lobsters   shrimp

squid   octopus   salmon   tuna

flounder   haddock   red snapper

tilapia   catfish   trout   bass

Seafood is a term that includes fish, **shellfish**, and other animals that live in water. Shellfish (clams, oysters, and scallops) are removed from their shells, and they are often covered with a **batter** of flour, milk, and eggs and fried. Oysters are often eaten **raw** – not cooked. Two other favorite kinds of seafood are crabs and lobsters, covered from end to end by a hard shell that has to be **cracked** to get to the meat. Maybe the most common seafood of all is shrimp. Shrimp is also battered and fried and it is served in casseroles, salads, and as a popular appetizer, shrimp cocktail. For many people, the peculiar looking squid and octopus with their many arms are a favorite seafood. However, many others are turned off by these strange creatures.

There are dozens of kinds of fish, but a few are especially popular in the United States and Canada. Salmon, a fish that comes from the Pacific Northwest, is available fresh, **frozen**, canned, or smoked (lox). Tuna is available fresh, but it is also canned, and used as the main ingredient in a casserole or sandwich. Another **staple** among the fishes is cod, associated with New England and the Maritime provinces, and often caught and then frozen on factory ships in the Atlantic Ocean. Other popular fish are flounder, haddock, and red snapper. In a good fish market, you can see all of these and more, whole or cut up into **fillets** with the **bones** removed.

Many people prefer to buy **fresh-caught** fish – the fish has been caught just a few hours or days before it appears at the market. Others buy it frozen – when it is caught, it is immediately packed into an extra cold **freezer**. From there it is shipped frozen to markets all over the country. Some think it is as good as fresh, and it is very convenient because you don't have to worry that it will spoil. Another sign in the display case may be "**farm-raised**," meaning that the fish are grown in a fish farm and are not free and wild.

Not all fish come from the sea. Freshwater fish such as tilapia, catfish, and trout can be found in a supermarket. They are usually farm-raised, but they can also be caught by people who are fishing with a rod and reel for fun and for their own dinner. Bass are another favorite sport fish, caught mainly in lakes.

And then there is the rather strange sport called ice fishing in the northern states and provinces. People go out on a frozen lake, cut a hole in the ice, drop in a line, sit back on a portable chair in their home-made "ice shack," and hope. (454)

I. Match the phrase on the left with a phrase on the right.

1. Not all seafood _____	A. watch out for the bones.
2. Shellfish are not _____	B. a liquid.
3. Batter is _____	C. does not have bones.
4. A raw oyster _____	D. you have to crack the shell.
5. To open an egg _____	E. comes from the sea.
6. Some fish are frozen _____	F. of trout and bass.
7. A staple food _____	G. actually fish.
8. A filleted fish _____	H. is not cooked.
9. When you eat fish, _____	I. are raised by fish farmers.
10. If it is fresh-caught, _____	J. it has not been frozen.
11. The freezer is full _____	K. on factory ships at sea.
12. Farm-raised fish _____	L. is a basic, important food.

II. Fill in the blanks with a form of the key word.

**seafood   raw   staple   fresh caught   shellfish   crack
fillet   freezer   batter   frozen   bony   raised**

1. Let's put the flounder in the _____ .

2. To fry the clams we'll need some _____.

3. This lobster shell is hard to _____ .

4. I think _____ oysters are yucky.

5. Some fish are very _____ . Be careful when you eat them.

6. I don't want the salmon steak; I'll have the _____.

7. The cod fish is a _____ fish in the Northeast.

8. My favorite _____ is scallops.

9. My brother hates _____ ; he eats only meat.

10. Catfish are often _____ in very large farms.

11. I will not eat _____ fish; only _____ for me!

Answers on 122

III. Fill in the blanks with a form of the key word.

1. Fish _____ can get stuck in your throat.
2. Rice is a _____ food in Asia.
3. This bowl has a _____ in it. Throw it away.
4. It was _____ just two hours ago.
5. Legal _____ s is a famous fish restaurant and market in Boston.
6. Although clams are called a _____, they don't swim.
7. The _____ we use for frying clams is based on a secret recipe.
8. The fish in sushi is _____.
9. The _____ is full of frozen food.
10. This fish farm _____ tons of salmon.
11. I forgot to take the flounder out; it's still _____.
12. Do you know how to _____ a trout?

IV. Fill in the blanks with a form of the key word.

Welcome to Captain Stark's _____ Restaurant. Here in Portsmouth, fish

is a basic dietary _____ . Today our _____ special is scallops in

a cream sauce. Our lobsters are _____ – right out of the trap. We

serve them all _____. Just pick out the meat. Our fried clams are soaked in

a thick buttery _____. They're crisp and crunchy. The only item from our

_____ is the calamari imported from Greece. Our salmon is _____

raised, but never _____. It's very fresh. We have a _____ bar with

sushi and oysters on the half _____ .

If you're up to eating octopus, I can guarantee there are no _____ to

worry about. And finally, let me personally recommend our baked haddock

_____. It's cooked with a great garlic and cream sauce.

Thanksgiving

bread   onions   vegetables   juice   fruit
kidney   liver   potato   milk   squash
peas   broccoli   cranberry   apple
pumpkin   raisins   venison

The best known traditional meal of the United States comes at Thanksgiving, the fourth Thursday of November. Thanksgiving began in the seventeenth century with the early settlers of Massachusetts who, with the help of the Indians, survived their first year in the New World. The settlers celebrated their first **harvest** by dedicating a feast of thanksgiving to God. They now had hope that they could make a new life in North America.

At that time, one of the common wild birds was the turkey. Today people eat **domesticated** turkey at Thanksgiving. The turkey is **roasted** for several hours in an oven. It has to be watched and **basted** from time to time – the juice must be spooned over the outside to keep the turkey from drying out. The inside of the turkey is stuffed with **stuffing** (some people call it dressing), a mixture of small pieces of bread, spices, onions, and other cut-up vegetables.

After the saying of **grace** (a short prayer given at the beginning of a meal), the Thanksgiving **feast** begins. First, there is a juice or fruit appetizer. Then the main course begins with the carving of the turkey. One person cuts off slices of meat. Turkey gravy, made with the juice of the turkey, flour, and sometimes the kidney and liver, is put on top of the mashed potatoes with a **ladle**, a large, deep spoon. **Creamed** onions, cooked in a liquid made from flour and milk, are also popular. Squash is another traditional Thanksgiving vegetable, and most people add something green like peas or broccoli.

Cranberry sauce is very traditional. It is made from a slightly sour red berry that used to grow wild in coastal New England. Today it is **cultivated** mainly in Wisconsin and Massachusetts and several Canadian provinces, especially in British Columbia. For dessert there are pies: apple, squash, and pumpkin are often associated with Thanksgiving. There is also mincemeat pie, a mixture of finely chopped (**minced**) pieces of meat with fruit, raisins, and spices. In the days of the Pilgrims, as the early settlers were called, the meat was venison – wild deer meat.

Nowadays, after the meal, many people retire to the living room to watch a newer tradition on television – Thanksgiving Day football games.

Canada's Thanksgiving holiday, a celebration of the fall harvest, has been celebrated on the second Monday in October since 1957. Similar to the American holiday, it features parades, football, and turkey. For many Canadians it is a last chance for a long weekend before the winter sets in, although in Quebec and the Maritime provinces it is not as important as it is in the rest of Canada. (443)

I. Match the phrase on the left with a phrase on the right to form a sentence.

1. The harvest _____	A. the turkey for four hours.
2. We had a feast _____	B. to serve the gravy.
3. The domesticated turkey _____	C. to say the grace.
4. We roasted _____	D. was done in the fall.
5. To keep the turkey moist _____	E. you must baste it.
6. I like to add walnuts _____	F. is often eaten as a pie at Thanksgiving.
7. Let's ask Grampa _____	G. are prepared with a white sauce.
8. I'll now begin _____	H. to the stuffing.
9. Use the ladle _____	I. are grown by farmers.
10. Creamed vegetables _____	J. to carve the turkey.
11. Cultivated crops _____	K. that lasted for over an hour.
12. Mince meat _____	L. is bigger than the wild turkey.

II. Fill in the blanks with a form of the key words.

harvest   feast   Domesticated   roasting   baste   stuffing
grace   carving   ladle   creamed   Cultivation   minced

1. The _____ knife must be very sharp.

2. Some families say _____ at every dinner.

3. The word _____ is related to "festival."

4. _____ is the process of growing food crops.

5. _____ animals are not wild.

6. Garlic that is chopped into very small pieces is _____ .

7. I will _____ the turkey every half hour.

8. Put the _____ into the turkey before _____ it.

9. The Canadian Thanksgiving celebrates the fall _____ .

10. You can use the _____ for serving the _____ onions.

Answers on 122

III. Use the key words in the blanks below.

1. The word "_____" is derived from the Latin "gratia" for thanks.
2. If you don't _____ the turkey it will become rather dry.
3. A _____ is a kind of big spoon.
4. You can make your own _____ with dried pieces of bread.
5. You can buy a hot, _____ chicken at that grocery store.
6. Human beings have _____ many wild animals.
7. I love _____ of mushroom soup.
8. The _____ of rice began in China a few thousand years ago.
9. Something that is finely chopped is _____ .
10. Every kitchen should have a _____ knife.
11. The _____ of Lupercal is on February 15th.
12. The pumpkin _____ was very good this year.

IV. Use the key words in the blanks below.

AAB: Dr. Know, what is Thanksgiving?
Dr.K: Basically, in America it was a _____ held by the first settlers of Massachusetts. They celebrated the _____ of crops such as squash, potatoes, and pumpkins. And the main course was often the turkey – not our huge _____ turkeys but wild turkeys that were plentiful then. And their vegetables were not as big as our _____ carrots and potatoes. They also baked pies using fruits and _____ deer meat. They were thankful for the successful harvest and I am sure they expressed their thanks by saying _____ before the feasting began. It's still a tradition.
The Canadian Thanksgiving is similar, but it is based on other traditions, and is thought of as a harvest celebration.
AAB: And what is your secret for _____ the turkey?
Dr.K: There is no secret, but _____ the turkey every ten minutes in its own juices is necessary. And I insist on _____ my turkey with dried bread, herbs and spices, and a few cranberries.
AAB: My mouth is watering. I can almost taste that first slice of white meat _____ from the breast, and piping hot gravy _____ onto the potatoes with a huge bowl of _____onions.
Dr.K: And don't forget the cranberry sauce.

Cookouts

meats   beer   iced tea   potato chips   nachos

salsa   vegetables   steak   hamburgers   hot dogs

chicken   onion   green peppers   shish kebab

corn on the cob   strawberry shortcake   cream

ice cream   clams   lobsters   seafood

When the weather is warm, many families enjoy a cookout in the yard with a portable grill. Some **grills** operate on gas, but the traditional grill uses small blocks of partly burned wood called **charcoal**. People like eating outside because they enjoy the taste of charcoal-broiled meats, as well as the experience of eating in fresh air.

Cold drinks go naturally with cookouts. Beer, iced tea, and soft drinks are usually available. While waiting for the charcoal to become hot, people drink and eat appetizers such as potato chips with sour cream **dip**, nachos (corn chips) with salsa, and even raw vegetables for those who are worried about calories.

Steak, hamburgers, hot dogs, and chicken are the meats that are most commonly charcoal-broiled. Sometimes small chunks of meat, onions, and green peppers are prepared as a shish kebab, on a long metal stick called a **skewer**. Another favorite food is corn on the cob. The ears of corn are dropped into hot water and removed after just a few minutes. The kernels are buttered and salted and stripped off the cob in mouthfuls.

Strawberry shortcake is a favorite summer dessert. Partially **crushed** strawberries are placed between the two halves and on top of a small vanilla cake. Cream that has been beaten to a light, smooth topping – **whipped** cream – is added to the top. Of course, another summer favorite is ice cream.

The **clambake** is a special kind of cookout that is done at the seashore. A fire is built in a **pit**, and rocks in the pit are heated. The rocks are covered with a layer of seaweed. Clams, lobsters, and other seafood are put on top of the seaweed, and the whole thing is covered with a heavy cloth to keep the heat and moisture in and bake the seafood.

A **barbecue** is another kind of outdoor event. The original kind – made famous in the American West – is a cookout in which a single, large piece of meat is roasted on a **spit**, a metal rod, over an open fire. The spit is turned slowly so the meat roasts evenly. Barbecues, like clambakes, can also be done in a pit.

Foods are associated with different sports; baseball has hot dogs, for example, but American football has a different tradition – **tailgating**, a tradition that is beginning to catch on in Canada. Before a game, which is usually on a weekend afternoon in the fall, people gather on the stadium parking lot to eat hamburgers and talk about the game. The food is typically laid out at the tailgate of a small pickup truck. Someone brings a grill. There are drinks, chips, nachos, and maybe corn on the cob. When it's game time, the tailgate is closed and people head into the stadium where, if they are still hungry, they can get food from **vendors**. (477)

I. Match the words on the left with those on the right to form a sentence.

1. Some portable grills _____   A. at the seashore.
2. Partly burned wood _____   B. use a skewer.
3. Sour cream is _____   C. are used for barbecued meat.
4. A pit _____   D. can be roasted on a spit.
5. To make a shish kebab, _____   E. use gas.
6. Crushed ice _____   F. is called charcoal.
7. Whipped cream _____   G. can be put in soft drinks.
8. Clambakes are held _____   H. the basis for a dip.
9. Special sauces _____   I. on city streets.
10. Large pieces of meat _____   J. as a table.
11. A tailgate is used _____   K. is a hole in the ground.
12. You may see vendors _____   L. is used on desserts.

II. Fill in each blank with a form of a key word.

**grill   charcoal   dip   pit   skewer   crush   whipping
clambake   barbecue   spit   tailgate   vendor**

1. After you open the can of _____, you should keep it in the fridge.

2. You can buy _____ cream and make it yourself.

3. We bought lobsters and clams for the _____ .

4. To light the _____, you should use a starter.

5. Let's put the grill up on the _____ .

6. Don't _____ the strawberries completely.

7. He makes good money as a hot dog _____ .

8. A _____ barbecue is done by putting the food in a hole in the ground.

9. A charcoal _____ does not use gas.

10. It's your turn to turn the _____. I'm tired.

11. Will you _____ these vegetables for the vegetarian shish kebab?

12. His _____ sauce is well known in this area.

Answers on 122

III. Fill in each blank with a form of a key word.

1. A cookout can be a _____ at the seashore or _____ at a football game.
2. I make my own _____ with sour cream and cheese spread.
3. Would you like some _____ cream on your pie?
4. We used _____ ice to keep the meat cold.
5. There's an ice cream _____ over there! Let's go!
6. My hands are dirty because I have been handling _____ .
7. I bought a charcoal _____ for $30.00.
8. At a _____ barbecue the food is put in the _____ and then covered over.
9. A whole pig can be roasted on a _____.
10. Put the _____ sauce on while it is roasting.
11. We need ten _____ for the shish kebab.

IV. Fill in each blank with a form of a key word.

Dear Mom,

I'm having a great time at Uncle Mike's. Yesterday we went to the beach and had a _____ . I helped dig the _____ . Believe it or not, I even ate some raw vegetables with a seafood _____ . There was also a bunch of _____ there, and I had some popcorn and ice cream. Tomorrow we're going to roast a side of beef on a _____ . And Saturday we take his pickup to the Michigan-Ohio game for a _____ party. I'm making the shish kebab and we're doing 15 _____ . And at home, last Tuesday, Uncle Mike _____ some pork with Aunt Mabel's _____sauce on his portable _____ _____. It was fantastic ! And I had three strawberry shortcakes with a ton of _____, juicy strawberries and we used a whole can of _____ cream.

Do you think I'm eating too much?

Love,

Jackie

LESSON 12
Picnics

chips   hard-boiled eggs   apples   cheese

pickles   beer   lemonade   apple cider

salt   pepper

Cookouts are fun, but many people like to get closer to Mother Nature and have a picnic in the countryside. State, provincial, and local governments, the U.S. Forest Service, and Parks Canada maintain picnic areas at natural spots by a river, lake, or seashore or on a mountain highway. Picnic areas may be free, but some of them may charge a fee. They often offer picnic tables, fireplaces, and toilets.

In addition to bringing food, some essentials for picnickers to bring may be: a **picnic basket** for the food, a **blanket** for the ground if there are no tables, a **tablecloth** if there is a table, and a **cooler** for the drinks. Some people will bring a **camp stove** for cooking things. It uses a canister of propane gas. For a simpler picnic, sandwiches are the main thing. Chips, dip, and hard-boiled eggs are also easy to take, along with an apple and maybe some cheese and pickles.

The usual drinks are bottles or cans of **soft drinks** and beer or a **jug** of lemonade in the summer, and apple cider in the fall.

Paper **napkins,** along with some salt and pepper and plasticware, are almost a necessity. And when it's over, look for the recycling bin. Nowadays, many people take their **garbage** home for **composting**. The process of composting begins with garbage collected in a special bin and then taken to a facility where it is turned into compost, a valuable soil for growing more food. Many communities pick up garbage for composting along with recyclable materials and trash.

It may not be a bad idea to bring bug spray. Ants, flies, and wasps are always on the lookout for free food. And mosquitos are looking for you.

And then there is roadside camping in campgrounds. In these places you can put up a tent or park your camper. Some people like to go deeper into the forest and choose to backpack, carrying all their needs on their backs. Obviously, they cannot easily carry heavy cans of food or fresh food that needs refrigeration. For these people, packages of **dehydrated** food are a necessity. They too, may be bothered by bugs, but they may also be bothered by bears if they do not put their food into a strong sack and hoist their food on a rope high into a tree.

Whether on a picnic, at a campground, or in the wilderness, or even on a city sidewalk, **alfresco** dining, eating outside in fresh air, is becoming more and more popular. (422)

I. Match the words on the left with the appropriate words on the right to make a sentence.

1. A picnic basket _____	A. of cider will serve several people.
2. A blanket _____	B. is Italian for "in fresh air."
3. A tablecloth _____	C. are useful for keeping our hands clean.
4. A cooler _____	D. is used for carrying the food.
5. A camp stove _____	E. food does not weigh very much.
6. Soft drinks _____	F. is put on the ground.
7. A jug _____	G. can be turned into compost.
8. Napkins _____	H. is used to keep food and drinks cold.
9. Garbage _____	I. can be used as soil for growing things.
10. Compost _____	J. are non-alcoholic juices and sodas.
11. Dehydrated _____	K. uses propane gas.
12. Alfresco _____	L. is nice to have if the table is dirty.

II. Fill in each blank with a form of a key word.

picnic basket   blanket   tablecloth   cooler   camp stove   jug
soft drinks   napkins   garbage   compost   dehydrated   alfresco

1. Let's go _____ tonight. Eat under the stars.

2. You drank that whole _____ of cider? I can't believe it!

3. I think this _____ is not very good; the food is warm.

4. I'm glad we brought a _____ . This table is very dirty.

5. Our _____ _____ is full. We can't take more food.

6. I don't think _____ meals are so bad.

7. We put our _____ into the _____ bin.

8. Paper _____ are very useful.

9. Don't forget to bring some _____ _____ for the kids.

10. We won't need the _____; there's a table.

11. It would be nice to have a _____ _____, but let's just take

   sandwiches.

Answers on 122

III. Fill in each blank with a form of a key word.

1. We brought only _____ _____. No beer.
2. It's always good to have a large _____ of water.
3. I'm afraid I forgot the paper _____ .
4. The _____ _____ is out of gas.
5. We have a _____ pit in our yard for
   our _____ .
6. Some _____ meals for backpackers are quite tasty.
7. We need to buy some ice for the _____ .
8. They have picnic tables there; we won't need a _____ for
   the ground.
9. That's my best _____. Don't put it on that dirty table.
10. Yeah, dining _____ is great when it isn't raining.
11. Oh, no! We left the picnic _____ back at the picnic area.

IV. Fill in the blanks with a form of a key word.

Hi Pat,

   You missed a great picnic. When we got there, all the tables were taken. So we just spread the _____ on the ground, right?
Problem; no _____ .

   OK, so we used the _____, only it wasn't big enough for all of us, so I sit on the ground and get stung by a wasp.

   Then Andy dropped the _____ and the _____ _____ are all over the ground. And the _____ of lemonade breaks and everything is covered in lemonade. We moved to a different spot.

   I decide to cook the hot dogs, but there's no gas for the _____ _____. Never mind, we do have sandwiches in the picnic _____, right? Yes, we do, and by then the basket is full of ants.

   I tried to light a fire in the fireplace and burn up all the _____ trying to get it going. So we came home with lots of _____ for the _____ pit, and had a package of _____ beef stew for dinner.

   That was an _____ experience I'd rather forget.

                                                    Bill

Fast Food: For Here or to Go?

potato salad   hamburger   cheese   bread   bun

roll   relish   ketchup   mustard   onion

tomato   lettuce   French fries   poutine   milk

milkshake   chocolate   vanilla   strawberry

hot dog   sausage   fried chicken

fish and chips

For people in a hurry, lunch is often a stop at a fast-food restaurant, at the take-out counter of a **deli**, or at a **food cart**. At some fast food restaurants, people just barely stop. They use the drive-through. They order and pay for it at one spot and then drive a few feet to a window where they pick up their food. In a city, people pop into a deli and pick up a **ready-made** sandwich and some potato salad. Or they may stop at a food cart on a street corner, and leave with a sandwich and a drink that they can take back to their office.

The ground beef patty, better known as the hamburger, is probably the most popular fast food. If it is grilled with a slice of cheese on top, it is called a cheeseburger. The hamburger is served on a round piece of bread called a bun or roll. People add a variety of **condiments,** such as relish, ketchup, mustard, onion, tomato, and lettuce.

Fries, also called French fries, are another fast food specialty. Potatoes are sliced into strips, put into a basket, and then deep-fried in very hot oil. Fries are eaten with the fingers, leaving the fingers slightly **greasy**. A favorite in Canada is poutine, fries topped with gravy and cheese.

For a beverage, there is a small carton of milk, or soft drinks in cans or paper cups containing crushed ice. Soft drinks come in dozens of types, including diet drinks with no calories. In addition, bottled water is popular. Milk is the basis for the famous milkshake. A flavoring (usually chocolate, vanilla, or strawberry) is added to the milk, along with ice cream, and the mixture is mixed in a high-speed mixer. All of these drinks can be served in paper containers with **lids** covering the top. A **straw** may be inserted through the lid and the drink can be sipped.

There are other fast foods. The hot dog is one. Just as the hamburger is not made from ham, the hot dog is not made from dogs. For almost all Americans, dog meat is not only **unappetizing**, it is repulsive. The hot dog is a sausage, and it is served in a hot dog bun. The hot dog is either grilled or **steamed** – cooked in a covered pot with just a little water.

Fried chicken from the southern part of the United States, tacos from Mexico, and fish and chips from Britain are also favorite fast foods. British chips, by the way, are the same as American fries. **Wraps** are a fairly new type of fast food. Meat, vegetables, and condiments are stuffed inside a flour tortilla or flatbread and neatly rolled up into a kind of tube.

Fast food places keep their prices down by serving in high volume and by giving customers **disposable** utensils such as plastic knives, forks, and spoons, and paper cups and plates to be **recycled**. (493)

I. Match the phrase on the left with a phrase on the right to form a sentence.

1. Deli is short for _____   A. tastes better than it looks.
2. There is a food cart _____   B. is ready to go.
3. Ready-made _____   C. are plastic.
4. Where are the _____   D. is a healthy fast food.
5. Don't put _____   E. delicatessen.
6. I can't find the right size _____ F. steamed or grilled?
7. Nowadays straws _____   G. on the corner of the street.
8. That unappetizing dish _____   H. lid for this cup.
9. Do you like your dogs _____   I. condiments? I need some ketchup.
10. A veggie wrap _____   J. your greasy fingers on my napkins.
11. Everything on this tray is _____ K. disposable, but not all of it is recyclable.

II. Fill in each blank with a form of a key word.

Deli   food cart   ready-made   condiments   greasy   lid   straw   unappetizing   steamed   wrap   disposable   recycled

1. Art's Cart offers only _____ hot dogs.

2. A place that does mostly fried food is called a _____ spoon.

3. Kids love to sip their drinks noisily with a _____ .

4. The _____ came off and I spilled my drink on my new pants.

5. There is no mustard on the _____ table.

6. This paper cup is made of _____ paper.

7. These _____ plastic utensils are not good for the environment.

8. To make a _____ you have to have some kind of flatbread.

9. The "Grab 'n' Go" section has _____ sandwiches.

10. Supermarkets now have a _____ counter.

11. Jose's _____ _____ offers burritos.

12. I just can't eat this; it's _____ .

Answers on 123

III. Fill in each blank with a form of a key word.

1. Do you remember that old song, "Sipping Cider Through a _____"?

2. This dish wasn't washed well; it's quite _____.

3. If you're in a hurry, get a _____ wrap.

4. The _____ for the cups are beside the plastic utensils.

5. Ahmed makes a great _____ at his _____ _____.

6. I like to _____ my vegetables; they taste better that way.

7. His new book, "The _____ Society" criticizes our wastefulness.

8. Have we got all the _____ for the cookout? Relish, mustard?

9. Our neighborhood _____ has kosher food.

10. This omelet is ugly and _____ .

11. Glass bottles can be _____ .

IV. Fill in each blank with a form of a key word.

Jon: Shall we take a break for lunch?

Sue: Let's order out. The Citi _____ is always good – and kosher.

Yoli: But there are some leftovers in the fridge.

Sue: Pretty _____, if you ask me.

Olga: I can just go out to the Streetwise Chef's for a _____ salad.

Jon: I'll buy that! He has great vegetarian _____ .

Hans: And great_____ sausages.

Yoli: But we don't have any _____. And I want mustard on my sausage.

Sue: Then you go over to Burger Queen for a _____ burger and a sugary soda.

And bring back some extra _____ and _____. We're all out.

Olga: Oh, why do we use straws? They don't _____ .

Hans: Why not? We live in a _____ world.

Coffee Shops

cream   sugar   latte   espresso
croissant   scone   jam   butter
biscotti   donut   muffin
tea   hot chocolate

The United States and Canada have had a revolution in coffee shops. In former decades, coffee was just part of a meal, usually breakfast. It was not the featured item. Then a couple of decades ago, small shops that sold special, **gourmet**, high-quality coffee began to appear. They succeeded. Now coffee shops are everywhere – in the city center, in the suburbs, and in the small towns.

Many types of coffee are found in coffee shops, and these shops compete with one another to give top quality. Plain coffee is the basic offering. It may be bought black (no cream), with cream, with or without sugar, or in any combination. It may be **regular** or decaf (no **caffeine**). Regular coffee contains caffeine, which is a kind of **stimulant** that wakes the body up. A lot of people want that morning jolt. Some don't, so they get decaf. Coffee may be roasted light (not so strong) or **dark roast**. Lattes, coffee with cream and sugar specially mixed, are popular, and so is espresso, a kind of concentrated coffee made with a noisy machine and served in a tiny cup.

Usually the **aroma** in a coffee shop is delightful, and the food, as well as the coffee, is tempting. Many **pastries** are served to accompany coffee – croissants (a flaky French pastry), scones (a heavier traditional British pastry that is split and served with jam or butter), and biscotti (a light and dry Italian sweet). Also, common American sweets like donuts and muffins can be found.

Some people take coffee very seriously. Every step of the process of making the coffee can be important to these people. Where do the **coffee beans** come from? Who were the farmers? How and when were the beans roasted? When were the beans **ground**? How many minutes ago was the coffee made? What kind of cup is used to drink the coffee? (Many shops even serve their coffee in a **mug** to cut down on paper waste.) Is the coffee organic? Some people seek answers to all these questions and more. Others just enjoy themselves without worrying. If you don't want coffee, the **barista** (a special name for the clerk) can serve you tea or hot chocolate, and cool drinks for the warm summer days. A coffee cooler, a mixture of coffee, sugar, milk, and ground ice, is refreshing.

The **atmosphere** of the coffee shop can be very important. Some shops are excellent places for doing work like writing or school assignments – people are chatting quietly, reading the newspaper, or working on their computers, taking advantage of the free wi-fi that most coffee shops have. Shops are great for socializing – groups are conversing about work or pleasure, parents are talking with their little children, students are conferring about problems at school. In any case, you will probably find comfortable chairs and tables, and you will be able to enjoy an hour or two for very little expense. (489)

I. Complete the phrase on the left with one on the right to form a sentence.

1. I used to drink ordinary
   coffee but _____   A. stimulant.
2. Regular for me, _____   B. in a big mug.
3. Caffeine usually doesn't _____   C. prepares espresso.
4. I usually buy _____   D. but not a lot of sugar.
5. A dark roast coffee _____   E. now I drink only gourmet.
6. I love the aroma _____   F. atmosphere in this shop.
7. My favorite pastry _____ G. of roasting coffee.
8. I like my morning coffee _____ H. keep me awake.
9. A barista _____   I. is a strong coffee.
10. I love the _____   J. is croissants.
11. Caffeine is a _____   K. beans, but today I bought ground.

II. Fill in each blank with a form of a key word.

**gourmet   regular   caffeine   stimulant   dark roast   aroma
pastry   coffee beans   ground   barista   atmosphere   mug**

1. You can smell the _____ of roasting coffee out on the street.

2. A good _____ makes a mean cup of latte.

3. I really like _____ with my coffee.

4. I gave my brother some really expensive _____ coffee.

5. Although I usually drink _____ coffee, sometimes I take it black.

6. Who broke my favorite coffee _____ ?

7. These _____ are from Vietnam.

8. I really enjoy the _____ in this place on a Sunday morning.

9. Did you know there is _____ in a cola and in tea?

10. A rich _____ _____ is a strong _____ for me.

11. I now _____ my own coffee with my new grinder.

Answers on 123

III. Fill in each blank with a form of a key word.

1. Mocha Joe's really has _____. It's small, warm, and dark.
2. I'm sorry, I don't consider a donut to be _____.
3. We are now importing _____ _____ from Cameroun.
4. My aunt is a _____ cook. Her creations are fabulous.
5. I never drink coffee in the afternoon. The _____ keeps me awake.
6. Ahh! The _____ of coffee. Where is it coming from?
7. The term _____ comes from Italian.
8. He has a collection of coffee _____ from all around the U.S.
9. The little pieces of ground coffee are called the _____.
10. _____ can mean ordinary, but in a coffee shop it means with cream or milk and sugar.
11. Alcohol is not a _____ .
12. My favorite _____ _____ is French roast.

IV. Fill in each blank with a form of a key word.

Journal entry. 2/07.

I saw Jack this morning at Dunn's enjoying a _____ of _____

_____ Sumatran. So, I joined him and ordered my usual daily shot of

_____ to get the day started. I had the _____ make me an

espresso, and I spent a few extra pennies on my favorite _____, a flaky,

sweet croissant. I really like the _____ there – quiet but busy. Laptops

and the *New York Times* everywhere. The scene _____ my sleepy

morning mind. What did we do before we had these _____ coffee shops

with the exotic _____ of roasting _____ from around the world filling

the air? No longer is it just Colombian. We have Asian, African, Mexican, not to

mention Turkish. That brought to mind those little cups of Turkish coffee with the

_____ in the cup. The coffee scene has changed since the days when the

only thing I drank was _____ Maxwell House.

International Restaurants on Main Street

| basil | chili | spice | garlic bread | guacamole | crepes |

Probably no countries in the world have a more diverse population than the United States and Canada. Here you can find almost every race, language, religion, and **ethnic** group. You can also find almost every type of food. Since the earliest years, people have arrived from all over the world, and of course they have brought their food with them. In the past couple of decades, immigrants have come in even greater numbers and greater diversity, and food choices have never been more available. For example, Toronto is often considered one of the world's most multicultural cities, and the list of international restaurants there is endless.

In every city, restaurants and grocery stores selling food from many international regions can be found. Adventurous eaters can explore **exotic** names of dishes and tastes new to them. Shops and restaurants specialize in a variety of ethnic foods . These **specialties** may be very **spicy**. The spices, like the people, come from many lands. Special spice shops sell everything from mild basil to hot chili. The aromas in these shops are interesting and **inviting**.

Some restaurants offering international food have been around for quite a while. For example, Italian restaurants in Boston, Chinese restaurants in San Francisco, Mexican restaurants in Texas, and French restaurants in New Orleans as well as French restaurants throughout Canada have been on the scene for more than a century. So garlic bread, sweet and sour dishes, guacamole, and Cajun dishes and crepes are **familiar** words to many people. But not everybody has **chopsticks** in their **silverware** trays.

Although ethnic restaurants can be **formal** or **informal**, most are informal. This informality makes it easy for people to stop in without making a **reservation**. Some or most of the **customers** may be speaking the language associated with the food, and there may be music to go with the food. If you don't know what ingredients a dish contains, you can always ask a waiter or waitress. Undoubtedly, they have answered the same question before.

The typical ethnic restaurant is a family business owned by recent immigrants, and some of the people waiting on you may be relatives of the owner. Two or three languages can be heard, and the menu may be multi-lingual.

If somehow people from previous generations could return to life, they would hardly believe the amazing mix of food to be found these days. So it is a good idea to take advantage of these opportunities. You can stay in your own city and take a food tour of the world. Or at least order Chinese **take-out.** (430)

I. Match the phrase on the left with a phrase on the right.

1. The only ethnic restaurant here _____   A. with chopsticks.
2. I like to travel to _____   B. quite spicy.
3. The specialty at Antonio's is _____   C. Mediterranean cuisine.
4. Thai food can be _____   D. when they bring chopsticks.
5. The appearance of this place _____   E. for take-out.
6. He eats only his old familiar _____   F. very best customers.
7. You can't eat soup _____   G. is Istanbul Kitchen.
8. I ask for silverware _____   H. is formal – jacket and tie.
9. The dinner tonight _____   I. exotic places.
10. I made a reservation _____   J. for four at six.
11. She is one of our _____   K. isn't very inviting.
12. I'll stop by Wong's _____   L. comfort food.

II. Fill in each blank with a form of a key word.

ethnic   exotic   special   spicy   inviting   familiar   chopsticks
silverware   informal   reservations   customers   take-out

1. My wife's _____ is very valuable.

2. The new place doesn't have many _____ .

3. The _____ tonight is spanakopita.

4. If you like _____ food, you'll love Bamboo Thai Restaurant.

5. I'm not _____ with Ethiopian cooking.

6. Do they have a _____-_____ menu at that place?

7. This city has more than a dozen _____ restaurants, from every continent.

8. You'll need _____ on Friday through Sunday.

9. Their menu looks very _____ . Let's go in.

10. Come as you are, it's _____ .

11. Could we have _____? It seems more natural with Chinese food.

12. The Shangri-La Palace looks very _____ .

Answers on 123

III. Fill in each blank with a form of a key word.

1. There's nothing _____ about Bob's Diner.
2. I called; we don't need _____ .
3. Don't take any _____. Plastic is good enough for a picnic.
4. That name sounds _____. Maybe I know her.
5. The _____ says it's _____ and potluck.
6. The _____ service desk is over there.
7. I dropped one of my _____. May I have another pair?
8. I hope my chili isn't too _____ for you.
9. Tonight I'm using Grandpa's _____ recipe for baked beans.
10. In my opinion, spaghetti doesn't qualify as _____ food.
11. This parking space is for _____-_____ customers only.

IV. Fill in each blank with a form of a key word.

COOKING FOR FUN WITH KATHY

This week we're going to take a stroll down Main Street and check out just how _____ our little town has become. You name it, and we've got it – well, almost. Panda's is no secret, I'm sure. Most of you are _____ with the big sign that says "TEA" that towers over the restaurant. And of course Panda's has lots of tea along with mild and _____ dishes, but ask for the _____. They assume we townsfolk don't know how to use them, so they bring _____ . At every lunch there are _____ at every table, and several people waiting for their _____-_____. And there are always some _____, like sweet and sour shrimp.

But if you're looking for something more _____, right in the middle of town we have the Shin-La (Korean), Bamboo Kitchen (Thai), Tulip Café (Turkish), and just a few yards up Canal Street, there is Three Stones Mayan cookery. When the warm weather returns and dining alfresco seems more _____, try the Jamaican food cart on the north end of town, very _____ – you can come in shorts, and no _____ are needed, ever. And with summer there's even more at the weekly Farmers' Market, where you'll find Thai, Malian, Indian, French, Mexican, and Chinese food.

The Brewpub

beer	**ale**	**stout**	**burger**	**fries**	**wings**

A few decades ago, people who loved beer used to say that they could not find any really good beer. You had to go to Europe to find memorable beer with real taste. In North America, beer was all made in huge factories, and it seemed **tasteless** and **weak**. Now that idea is gone, because small **breweries** make excellent beer, and they are found everywhere, in almost every city and town.

Brewpubs are bars that make their own beer or ale or stout, and they make it in small amounts, not like the giant factories that make it in huge vats. The beer is called craft beer and the breweries are called microbreweries. Brewpubs usually have their beer **on tap**, served in glasses or mugs. It is also called **draft** beer. It is brought to the bar in **kegs.** In the old days kegs were made of wood, but today they are metal. The keg is tapped (opened) and a plastic line brings the beer to the bar, where the **bartender** pulls on a long handle to fill the glasses. The glasses may be large (a pint) or smaller (a half-pint). The first few drafts from a newly opened keg may be mostly **foam**. Beer drinkers call the foam the "**head**." There is debate over just how much head is needed for the perfect beer.

Food, especially burgers and fries, is served in almost all brewpubs. Another favorite is Buffalo wings, which are actually chicken wings. Of course, buffalos do not have wings; they are called Buffalo wings because they originated in the city of Buffalo, New York. You can enjoy your burger or wings at a table, or at a **booth** if you want to have a more private conversation. If the pub is a **sports bar**, there will be many televisions tuned to sports shows. A lot of brewpubs have special parties on holidays such as Saint Patrick's Day in March. Sometimes green beer is served that day in order to honor Ireland and the Irish people. Other holidays might be celebrated at brewpubs, also. The biggest party is usually on New Year's Eve when at midnight everyone says goodbye to the old year and welcomes in the new one.

Brewpubs are great places to have fun with people you know or to meet people you don't know. Many customers are **regulars** from the neighborhood who already know almost everyone, but they are usually happy to welcome a newcomer, too. (412)

I. Match the phrase on the left with a phrase on the right.

1. This is tasteless; _____   A. we can watch the big game.
2. I don't like weak _____   B. than beer.
3. This brewery _____   C. should be about one inch thick.
4. On tap we have _____   D. coffee.
5. I prefer draft _____   E. should be enough for the party.
6. One keg _____   F. is 100 years old.
7. My favorite bartender _____   G. available?
8. This glass has more foam _____   H. I don't want it.
9. I think the head _____   I. beer and ale to bottled.
10. At Champ's Sports Bar _____   J. seven different ales and beers.
11. It's Friday; the regulars _____ K. will be coming in soon.
12. Is a booth _____   L. is on vacation.

II. Fill in each blank with a form of a key word.

**tasteless   weak   Brewery   on tap   draft   kegs
bartender   foam   head   booth   sports bar   regulars**

1. She attended _____ school to learn how to make drinks.

2. If you shake the bottle, you'll get lots of _____ .

3. They have over twenty kinds of beer and ale ____ _____ .

4. There are too many huge TVs in this _____ _____ .

5. Let's take that quiet _____ over in the corner.

6. We bought two _____ of beer for the party.

7. I think Mudd Lite beer is totally _____ .

8. I brewed my own beer, but it's rather _____. It looks like tea.

9. They have great _____ ales at Whetstone _____.

10. A beer without a _____ is like coffee without any aroma.

11. None of the _____ are here tonight.

Answers on 123

III. Fill in each blank with a form of a key word.

   1. As a _____ , I listened to many sad stories.

   2. I like a nice thick _____ on my beer.

   3. Can we get six people in this _____ ?

   4. That was a _____ remark. It offended me.

   5. There used to be a _____ there, but it burned down.

   6. That _____ _____ is a great place for wings.

   7. An empty _____ doesn't weigh very much at all.

   8. I really feel _____; am I getting a cold?

   9. I was there last night, but I didn't see any of the old _____.

  10. If it says _____ _____, that means it's _____ beer.

  11. If you shake it up, you'll get a lot of _____ .

IV. Fill in each blank with a form of a key word.

Those were the days, my friend. I used to be one of the _____ at

McSweeneys _____ _____. Everybody knew my name, even Nick,

the _____. Nick would keep those _____ nice and cold, and the

_____ on his ales was just right. That first pint was a beautiful sight, with

the _____ sliding down the sides of the glass. Nick's pints were great –

ten times better than that _____ stuff brewed at the huge Germantown

_____ over in Lagerville. I would drink three pints of Mickey's best

_____ ale, and then get a _____ with Paul and George and have

wings and tell _____ jokes. Last night I walked past, and that red

neon sign, Mickey's IPA _____ _____, brought back a few memories, my

friend. Yes, those were the days.

Supermarkets

fruit   vegetables   butter   milk   cheese   meat

soup   potato chips   corn chips   roast chicken

sushi   flour   candy

65

Most supermarkets are part of a chain of stores. The chains in the United States are regional, so for example in America you will find many Albertsons in the western states but not in the Northeast, where you will find Price Chopper. In Canada, Sobeys and Loblaws are found throughout the country. The third biggest, Metro, is found in Ontario and Quebec.

Supermarkets sell thousands of items – so many that sometimes finding exactly what you want can be hard. But if you know the various **departments**, you will not have a problem, though the number of choices can still be amazing. When you enter the store, the first thing to do is get a shopping cart or basket. Nowadays, many stores encourage you to bring your own **reusable** shopping bags. Then you begin your tour.

Each **aisle** of a supermarket may be a different department. The **produce** department contains fresh fruit and vegetables. The **dairy** aisle sells butter, milk, cheese, and other dairy products. And there are departments for meat, seafood, canned **goods** (products like vegetables, fruit, or soup, all in cans), and cereals. You can find aisles for frozen foods, and for snacks, such as potato chips, pretzels, and corn chips. There will probably be an area with **prepared foods**, where ready-made salads, roast chickens, or sushi can be found. There may be a **salad bar** where you can make your own salad. Some working people stop by the supermarket to get food for lunch, all prepared and ready to eat.

Many supermarkets have departments for ethnic foods (Mexican, Asian, Jewish, and so on), and you can always find an aisle for baking supplies, including many kinds of flour. Of course, supermarkets sell all kinds of other things. You can find pet food, napkins, vitamins, light bulbs, soap, and pills to help your upset stomach if you buy and eat too much.

When you **check out** (pay and leave), a **cashier** will help you, or you may use the self-checkout machine. The **scanner** will beep every time it records something you are buying. The scanner reads the **barcode** (a rectangle with many parallel lines) on the product, and it knows the price, even of items on sale at a special low price that week.

In many supermarkets you will be asked if you want "paper or plastic" if you didn't bring your own bags. You can choose what kind of bag you prefer. When your purchases are in bags, someone may help you carry everything to your car in the parking lot. No tips, please. (426)

I. Match a phrase on the left with one on the right.

1. A scanner reads _____   A. in my reusable bag.
2. At the salad bar _____   B. are ready-made.
3. You will find pretzels _____   C. check out.
4. Prepared foods _____   D. are in the produce department.
5. The dairy products _____   E. she can scan it.
6. Fresh vegetables _____   F. what's the price?
7. There is a hole _____   G. the barcode.
8. I don't usually buy _____   H. are at the back of the store.
9. I'm ready to _____   I. in the snack section.
10. There's no bar code on this; _____   J. there are lots of different olives.
11. Ask the cashier; _____   K. canned goods.

II. Fill in each blank with a form of a key word.

**department   Prepared food   reusable   aisle   produce   dairy
goods   salad bar   checkout   cashier   scanned   bar code**

1. This _____ is very fast.

2. I think this item was _____ twice.

3. You can find gum, candy, and magazines at the _____ .

4. Baked beans will be in the canned _____ aisle.

5. I love the _____ _____. It's so healthy.

6. In which _____ can I find croutons?

7. _____ _____ includes hot roasted chicken.

8. The store gave me three cents for each _____ bag.

9. There aren't many nice green bananas in the _____ department.

10. You'll find that in _____ six.

11. I really like the milk from Johnson's _____.

12. This product doesn't have a _____ on it.

Answers on 124

III. Fill in each blank with a form of a key word.

1. The deli department makes its own _____ _____.

2. A fresh salad at the _____ _____ makes a great lunch.

3. My uncle works in the meat _____ .

4. Fresh _____ can't be _____. It doesn't have a _____.

5. Are eggs considered a _____ product?

6. Suleiman owns a sporting _____ store.

7. A _____ shopping bag can last for a long time.

8. I'm sorry. This is the express _____ – only 10 things or fewer.

9. In the afternoon a lot of the _____ are high school students.

10. Paper goods are in _____ 13.

IV. Fill in each blank with a form of a key word.

I'm going to write a short story on my year in a supermarket. I worked in almost

every _____ . I collected shopping carts from the parking lot and spent

a few months at _____, first as a bagger; then as a _____.

I must have _____ every _____ in the place. I even

memorized the price of most of the items in _____. I stocked every

_____. I sold lots of _____ shopping bags to people,

telling them they need to think about the environment. I knew the exact location

of all the canned _____. I _____ my fingers stocking the

_____ food section and in the _____ products section I

dropped a carton of yogurt on my foot and broke my toe.

Tending the _____ _____ was my favorite thing to do. I had to

sample everything to make sure it was fresh. When I made _____

_____, I made some great wraps and sandwiches. I've seen it all, and now

I'll tell all to the world. Life at your local supermarket isn't easy.

Convenience Stores, Co-ops, and Farmers' Markets

milk   beverages   coffee   chicken

vegetables   lettuce   squash   butter   cheese

jam   maple syrup   honey   eggs

Most people do most of their food shopping at supermarkets, but not everyone gets their **groceries** at those big stores. Smaller stores meet the needs and desires of people in many different ways.

Convenience stores are often located on corners in heavily populated areas, so they're convenient to get to. And they tend to be open twenty-four hours a day. So, if you need milk or snacks or **beverages** at 3:00 a.m., the convenience store is there for you. They may charge a little more, but these mini-groceries offer a valuable service for people on irregular schedules.

Co-op markets usually serve a different kind of customer. They are not open all night, and they may not even sell the most popular soft drinks or a pack of cigarettes. They don't have bright neon lights, and they don't sell coffee in Styrofoam cups or soft drinks in 64-ounce containers. They try to offer natural and **organic** food products that have not been processed or grown with chemicals.

Those are some reasons why many people like co-ops. In addition, they are owned by members. In fact, some of the workers **stocking** the shelves may be members who are "paying" their membership fees by working.

A co-op may take ethical positions on social issues or food policy. Its members may decide that the co-op should stock organic food whenever possible, and use only **certified** organic **suppliers** of coffee. It may sell only **free-range** chickens and organic vegetables. It may buy from **local** suppliers or contribute part of its profit to a local charity. The customers are willing to pay more to support the co-op's policies.

When the weather is warm enough, in the spring, summer, or fall, all sorts of people flock to their local farmers' markets. These days, farmers' markets are in every town and in most neighborhoods of big cities. Usually, each one is scheduled for a morning or afternoon each week.

The food at farmers' markets is **seasonal** and local. It is fresh, **picked** or harvested recently, and usually grown by the seller. People who buy from a farmers' market are proud to be **locavores**. They buy and eat locally grown food to reduce transportation energy costs.

At a big farmers' market, you may see a dozen kinds of apples. In the spring, you may see five types of lettuce, and in the fall five types of squash. Any time of year, you may find farm butter and cheese, jam, maple syrup, honey, eggs, and much more – all local and delicious. And you have the added pleasure of supporting **growers** who are your neighbors. (434)

I . Match the phrase on the left with a phrase on the right.

1. We get most of our _____	A. have formed a cooperative.
2. If it's organic, _____	B. look for them in a cooler.
3. These strawberries were _____	C. are happy and healthy.
4. If you want cold beverages, _____	D. taste much, much better.
5. A convenience store _____	E. usually seasonal.
6. It takes a few hours to _____	F. supplies from a local supplier.
7. I think local veggies _____	G. your products certified as organic.
8. The apple growers _____	H. It is grown naturally.
9. Farmers' markets are _____	I. picked this morning.
10. Free-range chickens _____	J. carries groceries.
11. It's important to have _____	K. buys locally.
12. A locavore _____	L. stock all the shelves.

II. Fill in each blank with a form of a key word.

groceries   beverages   stocked   supplies   local   Free-range
certified   organic   season   pickers   growers   locavore

1. A _____ may or may not also be a carnivore.

2. These beans are _____ as organic and fair trade.

3. I buy almost all my _____ at SuperMart.

4. Although they sell _____, they don't sell beer.

5. The cold weather has hurt the orange _____ .

6. The apple _____ from Jamaica have arrived.

7. Summer is the right _____ for local strawberries.

8. We _____ the bread shelf this morning, and it's almost all gone.

9. Black River Naturals _____ our organic veggies.

10. Bronson's Egg Farm is _____ – just five miles from here.

11. _____ beef tastes better because the cattle eat grass.

12. More and more farmers are turning to _____ methods.

Answers on 124

III. Fill in each blank with a form of a key word.

1. The apple _____ need _____ workers. They are here about two months. They are also fast _____ .

2. A. J. Brown is a major _____ of _____ – soft drinks and beer.

3. We sold a lot of _____ yesterday; so that means we've got a lot of _____ to do.

4. It's not easy to be a _____ in the winter.

5. I know _____ meat and _____ food costs more, but I want to eat natural foods.

6. This stamp _____ that this meat processing plant has been inspected by the USDA.

7. "Eat _____" is a slogan that you will often see around here.

IV. Fill in each blank with a form of a key word.

I know, I know. Buying _____ fruit and vegetables costs more, and _____ chicken and eggs do too, but eating _____ organic food is better for you. And yes, our co-op can't buy huge quantities, so I pay more for my _____, and the _____ section is a bit limited; they don't have a lot of craft beer. But I enjoy being part of the co-op and putting in my weekly hours of _____ and cleaning. And I know that when corn is in _____, the coop will have it immediately. It will be _____ that morning at Miller's Farm and on the shelf 30 minutes later. You can't get more _____ than that! I even know some of our local _____ and _____, like the Hatfields with their wildflower honey, and the Silvestris who raise the best pigs in the county. So call me a _____. I'm proud of it.

The Kitchen

vegetables   carrots   potatoes   lemons   oranges

For many people, the kitchen is the most important room in the house. It is used two or three times each day, and people often find this hub of activity the perfect place to socialize. Even when other parts of the house may be more comfortable, a lot of people go to the kitchen to chat or help out.

Of course, food is prepared in the kitchen. **Recipes** tell you how to prepare it, and recipes require that cooks know how to **measure**, chop, **cut** things **up,** and do other things before the food is cooked. Each activity needs **equipment**. Measuring cups measure ingredients and come in fraction sizes like one-half or one-third. Measuring spoons include a **tablespoon** (Tbs), and a smaller **teaspoon** (tsp). After the ingredients are measured, they are sometimes put into a mixing **bowl**. This bowl is often part of a machine, a mixer, that thoroughly mixes everything. When not using a mixer, the cook mixes the ingredients by hand, often using a large wooden spoon.

A lot of things, like vegetables for example, need to be cut up. For that, there are big **knives** and little knives. Each kind of knife has its use. Bread knives are long and flat with a rough edge, and the multi-purpose chef's knife is big and heavy in order to cut thick things. The small **paring knife** is used for peeling and cutting small things. Many kitchens have all these knives and more to make the cook's job easier.

Preparing the food requires many tools, and here are a few that you will probably want to have. A peeler is used to peel vegetables like carrots and potatoes. A grater is used to grate things like carrots and cheese. Grating makes very small pieces and is often easier than chopping. A potato masher mashes potatoes to make the popular mashed potatoes. A rubber **spatula** is used to get all the ingredients out of a pot or bowl, so that nothing is wasted. And then there are all kinds of **gadgets** in the kitchen. Gadgets usually do just one or two things. For example, a juicer gets the juice out of lemons and oranges. They are not used every day, but they come in handy for a special job now and then.

Finally, most kitchens contain small **appliances** (machines) which may be on the counter or someplace in the cupboard. A food processor is popular, and so is a blender (for blending or mixing liquids) and a microwave oven, usually used to heat food quickly.

When the food is ready, it is served on the table, which has been set with silverware, glasses, plates, and napkins. Time to eat! (448)

I. Match the phrase on the left with one on the right.

1. This recipe requires _____	A. many knives.
2. It's important to _____	B. of salt too much for this recipe?
3. If you will cut _____	C. I rarely use is a juicer.
4. Isn't two tablespoons	D. up the carrots, I'll chop the onions.
5. Restaurant kitchen equipment _____	E. to get everything out of the bowl.
6. Put the ingredients _____	F. into a medium-size bowl.
7. The good kitchen has _____	G. a teaspoon of garlic salt.
8. A small paring knife _____	H. measure everything carefully.
9. Use a spatula _____	I. to sharpen knives.
10. This gadget is used _____	J. is useful for peeling apples.
11. A kitchen appliance _____	K. is sold at The Kitchen Store.

II. Fill in each blank with a form of a key word.

**recipe   measuring   cut up   tablespoon   teaspoon   equipment
bowl   knife   paring knife   spatula   gadget   appliance**

1. You'll need to mix these things in a _____.

2. A very important piece of _____ is the kitchen stove.

3. If you are going to bake your own bread, be sure to get a bread _____.

4. Mom's _____ for meatloaf is simple but tasty.

5. Use the _____ to peel the potatoes.

6. Oh dear, I used only a _____. Will that be enough?

7. Where is the _____ cup? I need it.

8. I need the celery _____ _____ into small pieces.

9. I find the _____ very useful for mixing things.

10. What's this _____ for?

11. You can find coffee makers in the _____ section of this store.

12. Tbs is the abbreviation for _____.

Answers on 124

III. Fill in each blank with a form of a key word.

1. Ay! I cut myself on that big _____. It's too sharp.
2. There are five _____ in my kitchen, and I need every one.
3. This handy little _____ is a garlic press.
4. Would you like a cup or a _____ of soup?
5. We have very little _____ in our summer camp kitchen.
6. Slice the cucumber; don't _____ it _____.
7. I can't make karne yarik without a _____. What is it?
8. Use the little _____ _____ for that.
9. I think the _____ is still in the mixing bowl.
10. _____ are bigger than _____.
11. Please _____ this cloth for me. I need exactly 36 inches.

IV. Fill in each blank with a form of a key word.

Welcome to Marisa's Kitchen. Today we'll talk about the basics for all you young men out there.

First, a little quiz to see what you know. Get out your pencils and write the answers. Question number one: What's the difference between a _____ and a tablespoon? Now, here are several sharp _____. Which one is the _____ knife?

OK, now tell me which of these things is the rubber _____ .
And here we have a _____ cup and a mixing _____.
Which is which? If the _____ says _____ _____ the carrots, what are you going to do? Chop? Slice? Mince? Grind? Grate? Or none of the above?

So, take a look at these _____. Which one is the potato masher? Now look at these two _____. Which one is the toaster oven and which one is the microwave? Well, if you didn't get that one, I understand. There is a lot of _____ in the modern kitchen. So, shall we check your answers?

Lesson 20

Health and Food

| dairy products | eggs | salt | nuts | bread | noodles |

77

Food is one of the best things about life. But like many good things, too much of it or wrong use of it can cause problems. These days, people have become more aware of **diet** and **nutrition** and how food can affect health.

One major problem today is **obesity**. Almost everything that is eaten or drunk contains **calories**, and if you eat more calories than you use, you will probably become very fat (obese) after a while. Today the obesity rate in the United States is higher than ever before, and it is becoming a significant problem in Canada. It is made worse by eating large **portions**, super-sized drinks, and **junk food**. Whatever the cause of obesity, obese people tend to develop more illnesses, including serious ones like **diabetes** and heart disease. Many efforts are being made to encourage people of all ages to eat fewer calories, control portion size, and get more exercise.

There are other problems with food besides obesity. Some people have an **allergy** to certain foods. They may be allergic, for example, to dairy products, to nuts, or to eggs. They may not know about their allergies, only that they sometimes get sick. Their doctor may have to do many tests to discover the problem and the connection between their allergy and its cause.

Some people suffer when they eat **gluten**, a substance found in many foods such as bread and noodles. These gluten-**intolerant** people must be careful when they buy groceries. They need to check the ingredients. Fortunately, most supermarkets today have gluten-free sections.

Many people want to know exactly what they are eating, so every food that is processed has a **label**. This label contains a lot of information. For example, the label will tell you all the ingredients in the product. It will tell you how many calories and how much salt the product has, when and where it was made, and many other things. A label is a gold mine of information. The product will also have a "Best By" date. After that date, the product is getting old and may lose some taste or nutritional value. Some products have a "pull date." This is the date when the store should pull the product off the shelf. It is too old to sell.

Though obesity and eating too much are very common, a few people have the opposite problem. People who have **anorexia** eat too little. They are so afraid of becoming obese that they develop a dislike or almost fear of food. People who are anorexic get too thin and can become very sick from not enough nutrition. So, here's some advice. Don't eat too much. Eat enough. Remember to eat nutritious food. Get plenty of exercise. Enjoy your meals. (459)

I. Match the phrase on the left with a phrase on the right.

1. My sister is on _____		A. is a good idea.
2. Nutrition is _____		B. is not fresh.
3. Obesity is _____		C. the result of bad eating habits.
4. It's a good idea _____		D. have anorexia.
5. Eating smaller portions _____		E. food allergies?
6. Junk food _____		F. on the label.
7. Obese people often _____		G. develop diabetes.
8. Do you have any _____		H. the study of food science.
9. "Gluten-intolerant" means _____		I. a gluten-free diet.
10. Processed food _____		J. to count your calories.
11. There's a lot of information _____		K. that consuming gluten makes you sick.
12. Some young girls _____		L. is not very nutritious.

II. Fill in each blank with a form of a key word.

**diet   nutritious   obese   caloric   portions   junk food
diabetes   allergic   gluten   intolerance   label   anorexic**

1. Her daughter is _____ because she eats very little.

2. His son is _____ because he eats too much.

3. Eat small _____ if you are trying to keep your weight down.

4. And watch your _____ intake.

5. A lot of fast food is really _____ _____.

6. I'm going on a _____ next week. Only vegetables.

7. You know, nuts are very _____ .

8. Yes, but I am _____ to nuts.

9. If you have _____, you have to watch your sugar intake.

10. Wheat flour is a source of _____ .

11. Did you read the _____ on that box of cereal?

12. A food _____ is an extreme sensitivity or allergy to a food.

Answers on 124

III. Fill in each blank with a form of a key word.

1. I love potato chips even though they are probably _____ _____ .

2. And there are a lot of _____ in chips.

3. On this small package, the _____ says 540 calories.

4. My son can't eat any wheat; he is gluten- _____ .

5. Do you have any food _____ ?

6. Not only is she _____, she has _____ .

7. Are you sure this product is _____-free?

8. She looks terrible. So thin! She must be _____ .

9. Eating small _____ is also very important for good health.

10. That salad may be _____, but I'm not sure about the dressing.

11. Dr. Wunderbar's low-carb _____ has helped me lose ten pounds.

IV. Fill in each blank with a form of a key word.

Dear Jennifer,

    I've just returned from two weeks at Dr. Wunderbar's Health Spa. I've already lost eight pounds following his special _____ . And I learned so much about eating disorders such as _____ and _____ . I've learned the importance of counting _____ and limiting food _____ . We also studied food _____, and how some people cannot have dairy products. Did you know that some people can get a very dangerous reaction to eating peanuts? And Jennifer, you really should stop eating _____ _____, like chips and Frosty Flakes. Not good for you! And avoid processed food, such as canned soups. Just look at the _____ on the can. There is more than mushrooms in mushroom soup. And avoid dairy products, if you are lactose _____. Yesterday we learned about how _____ is becoming more common because people are getting too fat, and how more and more people can't eat bread and need a _____-free diet.

    So let's do lunch at Mother Nature's Natural Kitchen.

                                  Paula

Vegetarianism

meat   vegetables   fruit   dairy products   salad
asparagus   peas   potatoes   squash   soybeans
rice   eggs   cheese   bread   wheat   chicken
turkey   pork   beef   lamb   butter

A lot of people have decided that they do not want to eat meat. Their reasons are varied. Some people believe that a vegetarian diet is healthier than a traditional diet; they think that they will live a longer and better life. Other people believe that eating meat is morally wrong; they think that humans should not use animals as food. These vegetarians may not like the way animals are treated on today's farms, or they may not want to make animals suffer. Finally, some vegetarians just prefer the taste of vegetables, fruit, dairy products, **grains**, and all the other things that can form a non-meat diet. Whatever the reason, vegetarianism is a popular **alternative** to a traditional diet in North America.

Of course, vegetarians eat a lot of vegetables: salads, asparagus, **greens**, peas, potatoes, squash, and so on. But they also eat many other things: **tofu** (an Asian food made from processed soybeans), rice and other grains, eggs, cheese, bread, **pasta** and all sorts of wheat products, and every kind of fruit. In short, many vegetarians eat just about anything that **contains** no meat or products made from meat (like chicken **stock**).

But there are various types of vegetarians. Some eat animals, but only certain types. Some vegetarians eat fish. Others eat fish and also **poultry** (chicken, turkey, duck) but not red meat (pork, beef, lamb). There are all kinds of combinations. A very strict type of vegetarian is a **vegan**. Of course, vegans don't eat meat, but they also don't eat anything that comes from an animal in any way. So they **avoid** milk, cheese, eggs, butter, and all other similar foods. Some vegans go so far as to avoid leather shoes and belts, because these things are made from parts of animals.

A small segment of vegetarianism is the **raw food** movement. Raw fooders believe that cooking damages the nutritional value of food, and they think that they can get more **vitamins** if they eat raw food rather than cooked food.

People on a vegetarian diet have a lot of choices these days. Large areas of supermarkets have sections for them, and most restaurants have vegetarian items on the menu. A few restaurants serve only vegetarian dishes, and this type of food is now seen as an ordinary part of people's diets. A hundred years ago, vegetarianism was often thought of as an odd part of society. Now big food companies are marketing food to vegetarians because, while still a minority, their numbers are a large economic force.   (421)

I. Match the phrase on the left with a phrase on the right.

1. Wheat and rice _____   A. are poultry.
2. An alternative to eating meat _____   B. is not cooked.
3. Spinach and lettuce _____   C. are vegans.
4. Tofu is made _____   D. is vegetarianism.
5. Spaghetti and macaroni _____   E. is like a thin watery soup.
6. Orange juice _____   F. are grains.
7. Chicken stock _____   G. contains vitamin C.
8. Turkeys and chickens _____   H. are greens.
9. Some vegetarians _____   I. dairy products.
10. Vegans avoid _____   J. are kinds of pasta.
11. Raw food _____   K. from soybeans.

II. Fill in each blank with a form of a key word.

**grains   alternative   greens   tofu   pasta   contain   chicken
stock   poultry   vegan   avoid   raw   vitamins**

1. Does this soup _____ any meat products?

2. The recipe requires eight ounces of chicken _____.

3. There are many _____ farms in the state of Maine.

4. My favorite _____ is lasagna.

5. We grilled a _____burger for you since you don't eat meat.

6. Rice, wheat, and oats are _____ .

7. She doesn't like _____, not even lettuce.

8. I'm sure this cheese is great, but I'm a _____.

9. It's difficult to _____ sugar; it's in lots of processed food.

10. There are no _____ in salt.

11. For a quick snack, _____ carrots are a great _____ to chips.

Answers on 125

III. Fill in each blank with a form of a key word.

1. Many people will eat eggs only from cage-free _____ .
2. Wheat, rye, and barley _____ gluten.
3. If you are allergic to wheat, the _____ is a gluten-free diet.
4. Spinach is a very nutritious _____.
5. Some people prefer the taste of _____ milk.
6. Do you take a multi- _____ pill every day?
7. My sister won't drink milk; she's a _____.
8. _____ is an alternative to meat.
9. There are many kinds of _____ in Italian cooking.
10. In addition to wheat, what are some other _____ ?
11. It's best to _____ fried foods.
12. To make beef stew, start with a can of beef _____.

IV. Fill in each blank with a form of a key word.

Washington (PLA) – A recent study by the V4U Institute has concluded

that _____ism, the extreme form of vegetarianism, is a healthy

_____ to a normal meat-based diet. The study involved 188 individuals

who agreed to _____ all forms of animal food products, including soups

made from _____. Of course no _____ was allowed, although

_____ , _____, and _____ were permissible. Spaghetti

and other forms of _____ were permitted as long as the dish did not

_____ cheese. Apparently the diet also provided sufficient amounts of

_____ A, B, C, and D. A similar study is being prepared for those who

follow a _____ food diet.

Cooking

hamburger   bacon   steak   vegetables

OK. You have the ingredients you need for your meal. You have the recipe ready. You have invited friends to your house, and in a few hours everyone will arrive. Now it's time to cook, and to cook well you need the right appliances and the right cooking methods.

A **stove** is essential. One of its main parts is the oven, where things like bread and pies are baked, and meat is roasted. Ovens contain metal **racks** that can be moved up or down, depending on the best place in the oven for the particular dish. The stove also has a **broiler**. That's where food is **broiled** – cooked by a direct source, not by hot air as in an oven.

On the top of the stove are the **burners**, which may heat with **electric coils** or **gas flames**. The burners provide the heat for cooking food on the stove top. A lot of things, such as hamburgers or bacon, are fried. Sometimes recipes say to **sauté** the ingredients – to fry very lightly. Some foods, like steaks, are **seared** before they are cooked. Searing is a type of frying, but it's dry, using no cooking oil.

The burners are also used for boiling food in water. Boiling something in an uncovered pot will cause the water to **evaporate**. If the pot loses all its water, the food will be burned. Often **simmering** is called for. That means the food should be cooked at or just under the boiling point. Some foods are steamed – they sit in a container above the water as it boils. The steam cooks the food. Nowadays many frozen vegetables are sold as steamables.

A good oven must be accurate, so that the food being baked will not be overdone or underdone. An oven **thermometer** is used to check the temperature. Many cooks also have a food thermometer that is stuck into the roast or bread to measure the interior temperature.

A couple of other very useful **devices** are the microwave oven and the toaster oven. Microwaves cook food very fast, and they are also good for other jobs such as thawing frozen food quickly. A toaster oven, small and portable, is good not only for toasting bread but also as an extra place to heat or cook food. Many people who live in small apartments like these devices, because they save space.

After all of your food has been baked, roasted, broiled, fried, boiled, simmered, sautéed, or steamed, your hungry guests will enjoy it.   (418)

I. Match the phrases on the left with the phrases on the right.

1. A stove has _____   A. with a blue flame.

2. There is a rack _____   B. is at the top of the oven.

3. Most stoves have four _____   C. evaporate when it is boiled.

4. An electric stove _____   D. an oven.

5. Gas burns _____   E. a useful device.

6. I sautéed _____   F. the vegetables very lightly.

7. Searing the meat_____   G. in the oven.

8. Water will _____   H. let it simmer for a while.

9. After boiling, _____   I. burners.

10. The broiler _____   J. oven thermometer.

11. We need an _____   K. has burners with coils.

12. A toaster oven is _____   L. will keep the juices inside.

II. Fill in each blank with a form of a key word.

**stove   rack   burners   coil   flames   sauté   sear
Evaporation   simmer   broiler   thermometer   device**

1. _____ is the process of a liquid turning into a gas.

2. Gas _____ are blue.

3. To _____ is to fry very lightly under low heat.

4. Before grilling, _____ the steak in a pan.

5. Turn it to _____ and don't let it boil.

6. A _____ can be electric or gas.

7. A mixer is a _____ I don't have.

8. One of the _____ on the stove top is not working.

9. When the _____ gets hot it turns red.

10. It's good to use a food _____ when cooking chicken.

11. Put the casserole under the _____ to brown it.

12. Put the turkey on the middle _____ in the oven.

Answers on 125

III. Fill in each blank with a form of a key word.

1. I like to cook my steaks in the _____.

2. Set the oven _____ for 350 degrees.

3. This _____ is great for steaming veggies.

4. Let's put that pot on the back _____ .

5. First _____ the vegetables very lightly; then add the shrimp.

6. Turn the gas down; the _____ are too high.

7. Let the stew _____ for a while, but don't let it boil.

8. Put the big pot on the larger _____.

9. When you _____ the meat, don't use any oil.

10. _____ milk has about 60% of the water removed.

11. This _____ has two _____ in the oven.

IV. Fill in each blank with a form of a key word.

A Little Word Play

1. There are many kinds of _____: for example, spice, wine, coat, hat.

2. He was angry, but he let it _____ until he blew up.

3. All his wealth _____ because of one very bad business decision.

4. Synonyms for _____ include char, scorch, and burn.

5. _____ is a word English borrowed from French.

6. An old _____ is a former boyfriend or girlfriend.

7. A snake is often seen _____ up like a bed spring.

8. Let's put it on the back _____ and discuss it later.

9. Once upon a time a _____ referred to a heated room.

10. They walked all day under the _____ hot sun of the Outback.

11. _____ is from the Greek language, meaning heat measure.

12. To devise (make) something is related to the word _____ – something

    that makes something.

Recipes

meat   cheese   carrots   vegetables

olive oil   beef   flour   butter   celery

salt   pepper   turkey   bread   crumbs

potatoes   lettuce   spinach   peas   onions

Y ou may have the best ingredients, the freshest fruit and vegetables, the finest **pots, pans,** and dishes, but your food will still probably not taste good unless you have a good recipe and know how to follow it correctly. Recipes tell you what to do **step by step.** Usually, at the top of the recipe, all of the ingredients are listed. It's a good idea to collect all of these ingredients before starting, so that you don't have to interrupt one of the steps later on.

Recipes use measurements, both **liquid** for water and **dry** for ingredients like **flour.** Here are some common liquid measurements:

a **quart**————32 ounces	a tablespoon
a **pint**————16 ounces	a teaspoon
a **cup**————8 ounces	a half teaspoon
a half cup————4 ounces	
a quarter cup———2 ounces	

Some recipes ask you to weigh dry ingredients (like flour or sugar). You need a **kitchen scale** that measures pounds and ounces to do this. Don't be confused by the word "ounces." It's a measure of weight (16 ounces in a pound) and it's a measure of liquid (8 ounces in a cup). Common dry measurements include cups and spoons.

You can learn a lot about how to follow these recipes by watching television cooking shows and from websites. There you can see professionals going through all the steps, and you can learn their techniques, such as the best way to **thaw** frozen meat. And you'll learn new words such as "**rinse,**" as in "Rinse the lettuce in cold water."

You'll find a lot of verbs in recipes, so let's review some before we go on:

Cut carrots into ¾-inch pieces	**Slice** cheese thinly
Mix ingredients in a large bowl	**Stir** mixture thoroughly
Mince vegetables and **sauté** in ½ cup olive oil	
Peel 8 ounces carrots and **dice**	**Thaw** beef and **roll** in flour
Spread soft butter over dough	**Fold** dough into thirds
Bake in a 360 degree oven	**Chop** two sticks celery
Add salt and pepper to taste	**Baste** the turkey every half hour
Coat with bread crumbs	**Melt** a ½ cup butter
Boil one cup water	**Fry** in very hot oil
Mash the potatoes (355)	

I. Match the phrase on the left with a phrase on the right.

1. A pot is deeper _____   A. in a quart.
2. Follow each step _____   B. it's not wet.
3. Water and milk _____   C. four liquid ounces.*
4. Flour is essential _____   D. than a pan.
5. If it's dry _____   E. rinse it.
6. There are two pints _____   F. carefully and don't miss one.
7. A half cup is _____   G. are liquids.
8. A scale is used _____   H. for weighing things.
9. After the turkey is thawed, _____   I. for baking bread.

II. Fill in each blank with a form of a key word.

**pot   pan   step   liquid   dry   flour   quart
thermometer   pint   cup   scale   thaw   rinse**

1. Milk is sold in _____ and gallons or half gallons.

2. She's on a _____ diet; no solids.

3. I'll wash if you will _____ the dishes.

4. This _____ is not very accurate.

5. The first _____ says to _____ the vegetables in cold water.

6. A frozen turkey takes several hours to _____ .

7. Obviously pancakes are cooked in a _____ .

8. We'll need a _____ to boil the water.

9. White bread is made with white _____ .

10. Beer is often served as a _____ .

11. This recipe calls for a _____ of chopped celery.

* also called "fluid ounces."

Answers on 125

III. Fill in each blank with a form of a key word.

1. Yesterday I bought a _____ of milk and a _____ of half-and-half.
2. I think I'll have a _____ of tea.
3. Many people now use _____ soap.
4. She really likes _____ Turkish apricots.
5. The bathroom _____ says I weigh too much.
6. To boil something you need a _____. A _____ is too flat.
7. The berries haven't _____; they're still frozen.
8. Has this spinach been _____ in cold water?
9. There are eight _____ in this recipe.
10. _____ is usually sold in bags.

IV. Fill in each blank with a form of a key word.

Ray's Beef Stew

Note: You don't need a _____; there's nothing to weigh.

1. _____ one. Gather all the ingredients; beef, potatoes, carrots, beef stock, flour, and if you like, peas and onions. For spices I like _____ (not fresh) dill and rosemary.
2. If necessary, _____ the beef if it's frozen.
3. Then _____ the beef in warm water.
4. *(Optionally)* Sear the beef in a hot frying _____.
5. Chop two _____ of carrots and four potatoes.
6. Pour the stock into a two-_____ _____.
7. Stir in some _____ to thicken the _____.
8. Turn on the heat. When the water is almost _____, add all the vegetables and the beef.
9. _____ the dill and rosemary and _____.
10. _____ over low heat for at least 30 minutes, _____ from time to time.

Will make two large bowls, or about two _____.

A Culinary Tour of North America

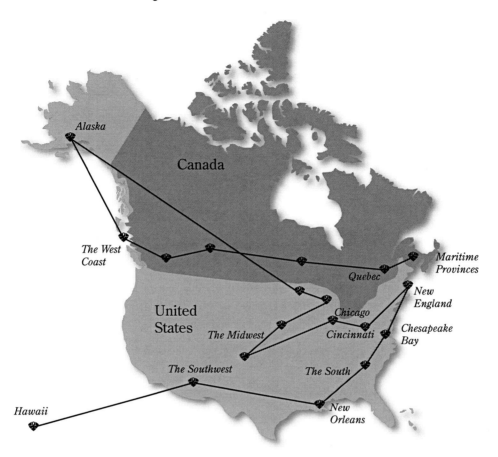

NEW FOOD WORDS

lobster roll   poutine   crepe   sucre a la crème
Montreal bagel   back bacon   Yorkshire pudding
pemmican   blueberry   cloudberry   king crab
walleye   Cornish pasty   hotdish   beefsteak
Boston baked beans   cheddar cheese   cornbread
soul food   turnip   tripe   gumbo   jambalaya
okra   crawfish   beignet   chili con carne
Navajo fry bread   poi   taro   Spam

Let's begin our tour in Canada's Maritime Provinces, where seafood is king. Lobster and cod are especially important here. A very popular lunch item is the lobster roll – lobster meat with mayonnaise in a bun.

Moving west we come to Quebec, Canada's French heritage province. Specialties here are poutine – a dish of French fries smothered in gravy and cheese curds. It is not a diet food. Another specialty is tourtiere, a spicy meat pie. Crepes, a kind of thin pancake often filled with sweet sauces, are also very popular here. And for dessert, sucre a la crème is made from sweetened milk. While in Montreal, try a Montreal bagel.

Across Canada, maple syrup and the maple tree are very important. In fact, the Canadian flag features a maple leaf. The syrup is collected from the sap of the tree and boiled until it thickens and becomes sweet. Almost everyone loves it on pancakes and waffles.

Canadians are fond of meat, and some national favorites are back bacon (Americans call it Canadian bacon), roast beef with Yorkshire pudding, and roast turkey. Bison, moose, and caribou are wild animals that Canadians eat. Native Americans make a dried meat called pemmican from these animals. Deer are commonly hunted for their meat, called venison.

Before moving to the west coast, let us mention that Canada is the world's leading producer of blueberries, along with other berries such as the cloudberry.

On the west coast, salmon is king – fresh, smoked, and dried. Now take a quick look northward to Alaska where the Alaskan king crab is caught. These crabs are giants – they weigh up to twenty pounds.

Turning back east through the United States and along the border, a favorite fish is the freshwater walleye. We'll also find shops selling Cornish pasty, a portable meal of meat and vegetables in a pocket of dough. To the south, in the Midwest, corn is everywhere in the summer, and in winter so is hotdish (a casserole made with starch, meat, and vegetables). And of course the Midwest is the heart of America's cattle industry, where the beefsteaks are big and fresh.

In the Midwestern city of Chicago, you are in the home of the deep-dish pizza, and in Cincinnati you'll find its famous chili.

Back east again, we are in New England with its seacoast on the Atlantic Ocean, meaning people eat a lot of seafood – clam chowder, cod, lobster, and fried clams. But the region is also noted for its Boston baked beans, and its many dairy farms that produce milk and the country's best sharp cheddar cheese. Vermont is famous for its maple syrup, and Maine for its potatoes.

South of New England, the Chesapeake Bay is proud of its own seafood, especially oysters and crabs. The Maryland blue crabs are often made into a delicious crab cake.

Farther south, we come to the land of southern cooking. This is where you find the best fried chicken and corn products such as cornbread and grits, a hot breakfast cereal. Here in the south, African-Americans created soul food, with its emphasis on greens, turnips, and animal parts like feet, ears, and tripe.

Going west brings you to the old city of New Orleans, where you will find unique dishes like gumbo (a kind of stew), and jambalaya (a mix of meat, seafood, spices, stock, and rice). Okra and crawfish are also special to this region. Those with a sweet tooth can try a beignet, the official state donut of Louisiana.

Next stop: the Southwest. Here barbecue cooking is very popular, and if you love peppers, you are in heaven. Meat, beans, and peppers are the basis for chili con carne. Mexican food is seen everywhere, and even has its own name: Tex–Mex. Native American foods are also found in this area: for example, Navajo fry bread.

Finally, there is one place you can't drive to – Hawaii. The common food includes poi (a dish made from taro root) and pineapple. You might want to go to a feast called a luau. It's a big event with roast pig, salmon, poi, tropical fruit, drinks galore, and entertainment.

Then there is Spam, and not the email kind. This lowly canned meat made in small towns in Minnesota and Nebraska is extremely popular in Hawaii and Micronesia. Why? The answer is that hundreds of thousands of military personnel have passed through the Pacific region over the decades. Spam was a typical meat for them, served for breakfast, lunch, and supper. Local people (in the United Kingdom and Australia, as well) developed a taste for it, so what had been the only choice for soldiers became the preferred choice for civilians. (781)

Better Homes & Gardens

Spice and Herb Chart

SALADS, VEGETABLES

Beets: Sprinkle in tarragon while they cook.

Cabbage: Cook with caraway or mustard seed.

Carrots: Season glazed carrots with ginger.

Cole slaw: Sprinkle with caraway or dill seed.

Corn: Flavor canned corn with chili powder; garnish with green pepper rings.

Eggplant: Add just enough basil or thyme to enhance flavor.

Fruit salad: Add allspice to whipped cream dressing.

Green beans: Add mustard to cream sauce.

Onions, creamed: Add mustard to cream sauce.

Peas: Drop in mint flakes or a pinch of savory while they're simmering.

Potatoes, mashed: Sprinkle in dill as you mash; or season with rosemary as they cook.

Tossed salad: Add curry powder to an oil/vinegar dressing.

BREADS

Biscuits: Add mustard and thyme to dry ingredients.

Blueberry muffins: Add a dash of nutmeg to dry ingredients.

Cinnamon Toast, French Style: Dip in egg, milk, and fry.

Coffee Cake: Mix anise in the batter. Just enough for taste.

Corn bread: Mix rosemary in batter.

Croutons: Toss toasted bread cubes with melted butter; season with onion, salt, basil, and marjoram.

Dumplings: Mix parsley flakes in the batter.

Garlic bread: Slice French bread partly through. Spread slices with butter seasoned with garlic salt.

Rolls: Add caraway seed to batter or put dill seed on top.

Scones: Season with allspice – serve with honey. Or mix poppy seed with strained honey.

Sweet bread: Add a pinch of saffron to hot liquid. Soak ten minutes; strain. Add to flour mixture.

Waffles: Add poultry seasoning, serve with creamed chicken. Or add a dash of allspice and cinnamon.

DESSERTS

Apple pie: Add cinnamon to crust.

Baked apples: Core and fill center with brown sugar, stick cinnamon.

Cherry pie: Add a dash of mace or nutmeg.

Chocolate pudding: Add a dash of cinnamon or mace.

Grapefruit: Sprinkle halves with ginger and coconut; chill to serve.

Peach pie: Sprinkle a dash of cinnamon to enhance the flavor.

Sugar cookies: Stir anise seed into dry ingredients.

Yellow cake: Add half teaspoon nutmeg and quarter teaspoon allspice to one package of mix

SOUPS, APPETIZERS

Beef soup: Add mixed vegetable flakes while it simmers.

Bloody Mary cocktail: Try a pinch of dill seed or a bit of oregano.

Chicken soup: Add a pinch of rosemary or a dash of paprika or marjoram.

Consomme: Season with allspice or a dash of savory.

Fish chowder: Cook with lots of vegetables, then add thyme.

Oyster stew: Add light touches of mace or cayenne.

Potato soup: Try a dash of mustard or basil.

Split-pea soup: Sprinkle in savory.

Stuffed celery: Mix caraway seed with cream cheese for stuffing; sprinkle with paprika.

Tomato soup: Shake in sage and garlic salt.

Vegetable soup: Add thyme or a dash of chili powder.

MEATS, FISH, POULTRY

Beef stew: Flavor with basil. Or cook with vegetable flakes or a dash of mixed herbs.

Chicken stuffing: Use poultry seasoning; or sage, thyme, onion salt.

Fish fillets: Sprinkle with marjoram, tarragon, or curry powder before cooking.

Fried chicken: Use paprika or sprinkle pieces with thyme and marjoram.

Hamburger patties: Add basil or curry powder.

Ham loaf: Mix in a bit of rosemary for flavor.

Hash: Add a pinch of marjoram or savory.

Meatballs: Season with savory, mustard, garlic salt.

Pork chops: Sprinkle with sage or thyme. Or add a shake of cinnamon.

Pork roast: Blend marjoram, savory; add to basting sauce.

EGGS, CHEESE

Cheese casseroles: Add a dash of sage or marjoram.

Cheese (Welsh) rabbit: Include basil and marjoram in the cheese sauce.

Cheese soufflé: Add basil to suit your taste.

Cottage cheese: Add onion, dill, or caraway seed.

Cream cheese: Blend in basil, or parsley flakes.

Deviled eggs: Add savory and mustard.

French omelet: Add a dash of basil in the eggs.

Scrambled eggs: Sprinkle lightly wth savory.

Tomato omelet: Add just a bit of oregano.

Source: Better Homes and Gardens

Sloppy Joe

1 lb ground beef
1 c barbecue sauce
1/4 c chopped green pepper
1/4 c chopped onion
6 hamberger buns
sliced American cheese

Brown meat; drain. Add barbecue sauce, green pepper, and onion. Cover. Simmer for 15 minutes. Spoon meat mixture on to the bottom half of a bun. Cover with slice of cheese and broil. Add top of bun. Makes 6 sandwiches.

Sloppy Josef

Add 1/2 lb sliced frankfurters and 1 cup dill pickle slices to the Sloppy Joe mixture. Cover bottom halves of Kaiser rolls with cheese slices; broil. Spoon on meat mixture. Serve with top halves of rolls.

Sloppy José

Add 8 1/4 oz can drained whole kernel corn to the Sloppy Joe mixture. Fill heated taco shells with shredded lettuce, meat mixture, and salsa. Cover with cheese slices cut into triangles.

Sloppy Joseppi

Add 1/2 c stuffed green olive slices, 1 tsp of dried oregano leaf, and some garlic powder to the Sloppy Joe mixture. Spoon onto Italian bread slices. Cover with strips of cheese; broil.

Sloppy Josephine

To the Sloppy Joe mixture add a 2 1/2 oz jar of mushrooms, drained and sliced. On the bottom halves of individual French rolls put slices of cheese; broil. Spoon on the meat mixture. Serve with top halves of rolls.

Casseroles

Traditional, Old-Fashioned Dishes from a New Hampshire Coast Ladies Aid Society

POACHED EGGS MAYONNAISE

3 shredded wheat biscuits	1 c hot white sauce
6 eggs, cooked medium	1/2 c mayonnaise

Split the biscuits, toast and butter. Put the crumbly biscuits into a casserole dish. Put an egg on each half biscuet. Season eggs with salt, pepper, and some dried herbs to taste.Fold mayonnaise into white sauce, and pour over the eggs. Serve from the casserole.

— Edith Warren

BAKED FISH

1 c flaked fish, cod or haddock	white sauce
2 hard-boiled eggs	1 c bread crumbs
butter	salt and pepper

Butter a baking dish. Put in layers of fish and bread crumbs until all is used, ending with a layer of crumbs. Put dots of butter on the crumbs. Sprinkle each layer with salt and pepper. Make a white sauce of 1 1/2 cups of milk, two tablespoons of flour, and 1 tablespoon of butter - cook slowly, stirring until smooth. Chop the eggs and add to the sauce, and pour over the fish. Bake in a 250 degree oven for 20 minutes.

— Helen Perkins

LAYER DINNER

2 c potato sliced	1 lb hamburger	2 green peppers
2 c onion sliced	1 can stewed tomatoes	cut up fine
2 c celery chopped	salt and pepper	

Butter a casserole. Mix hamburger into tomatoes. Put in layers of potato, onion, celery, and the hamburger-tomato mix. Salt and pepper each layer lightly. Sprinkle the peppers on top. Bake for 1 hour at 350 degrees.

— Minnie E. Philbrook

ONE-DISH DINNER

Put 4 tablespoons butter in a skillet, and fry 1 chopped onion and two sliced green peppers lightly. Add 1 lb hamburger, 1 tsp salt, and 1/4 tsp pepper, and mix well. Beat and add 2 eggs. In a buttered baking dish, put in 2 layers of 1 c corn, half the hamburger mix, and sliced tomatoes. Cover with bread crumbs and dot with butter. Bake 35 minutes in a moderate oven.

— Lillian M. Dearborn

PORK-POTATO CASSEROLE

6 pork chops, 1 inch thick	1 onion, coarsely chopped
4 tart apples, cored and sliced	1 c water
4 good-sized sweet potatoes	salt and pepper

Brown the chops in a hot frying pan and then place in a shallow casserole or baking dish. Season with salt and pepper. Peel and slice sweet potatoes. Arrange layers of potato and apple over the chops. Pour water over all. Cover and cook in 350° oven for 1 to 1 1/2 hours. Dark brown sugar sprinkled over apple and potato before baking gives added flavor.

— Bernice Campbell

Eggs Benedict

English muffin, split and lightly toasted
2 poached eggs, yolks runny
2 slices of Canadian bacon
asparagus, spinach, or other greens
Hollandaise sauce

Hollandaise: Melt a stick of butter - 1/2 cup. Put aside. Boil water in the bottom of double boiler. In top of double boiler, cook 3 egg yolks, beating constantly with a whisk. Add 1 tbsp of boiling water; beat until smooth. Add three more tbsp of water, beating. Add 1 1/2 tbsp of warm lemon juice, beating. Add a pinch of salt and cayenne. Put sauce aside.

Cook asparagus or other vegetable until just tender. Fry bacon lightly. Toast the muffins, Poach the eggs. Put a little Hollandaise on each half muffin, then put the bacon and asparagus on the muffin. Top with an egg. Spoon lots of sauce over the egg. Sprinkle with a touch of paprika and a fresh green herb - parsley, chive, dill. Serve with

Huevos Rancheros
Ranchstyle Eggs

This dish is popular all across the U.S. Southwest and everywhere around the world where Mexican food is enjoyed. There are as many recipes as there are cooks. Basically, on a lightly fried tortilla (corn or wheat; corn is traditional) spoon some sauce. On top put an egg, fried or poached. Garnish.

Here is one variation, a favorite. On the tortilla put some refried beans, chopped tomato, and chopped avocado, Over this spoon some fresh salsa, as hot as you like it. Then put on the egg, working quickly to keep the food hot. Sprinkle with fresh cilantro (or parsley, if you don't like cilantro). Sprinkly liberally with shredded Monterey Jack cheese or one of the similar, wonderful Mexican cheeses. Add a little chopped onion, a bit more salsa, and perhaps a dollop of sour cream. Serve with bacon or Mexican sausage, chorizo.

Or put the chorizo on the tortilla and serve the refritos on the side with some avocado and fresh tomatoes. Guacamole also goes well with huevos rancheros.

From
Salads
by Suzanne Best

Three-Bean Salad *(7 to 8 servings)*

A spicy, sweet-and-sour Southern favorite.

> 1 lb. each of green beans and yellow wax beans cut up and cooked until just tender
> or 1 16-oz. can each of cut green and yellow wax beans, drained
> 1 16-oz. can whole read kidney beans, rinsed and drained
> 1 medium green pepper, cored and cut in long, very thin strips
> 1 medium red onion, sliced crossways very thinly
> 2 cups cider vinegar
> 1/4 cup olive or other salad oil
> 2/3 cup of sugar, honey, or maple syrup
> 1/4 teaspoon cayenne
> 2 teaspoons salt

Mix the vinegar, sugar, salt, oil, and cayenne with 1/2 cup water until sugar dissolves. Place the beans and other vegetables in a large bowl or jar. Pour the marinade over them, cover, and refrigerate for 24 hours or longer. Leave any leftover beans in their marinade and nibble on them later.

Raw Mushrooms in Sour Cream *(4 servings)*

> 1/2 lb. fresh small white mushrooms
> 2/3 cup of sour cream
> 2 teaspoons lemon juice
> 1 1/2 tablespoon fresh dill (or chives), finely chopped
> 1/2 to 1 teaspoon salt
> several grindings of pepper

Combine the sour cream, lemon juice, salt, pepper, and 1 teaspoon on fresh dill (or chives) in a good-size bowl. Slice the mushrooms as thinly as possible directly into the dressing. Chill for an hour; the sour cream marinade intensifies the woodsy flavor of the mushrooms. Transfer into an attractive bowl for serving, and garnish with a smattering of dill (chives).

Avocado and Tomato Salad *(4 servings)*

South-of-the-border spice accents the delicate flavor of an avocado.

> 1 large avocado and 3 medium tomatoes cut into bite-size chunks
> 2 tablespoons minced onion

Make a dresssing of 1/4 cup olive oil, 1 1/2 tablespoons lemon juice, 1/2 teaspoon salt, and 8 or more drops of red pepper sauce. Add the avocado, tomato, and onion to the dressing and serve in a shallow bowl over a single layer of romaine, or other lettuce leaves.

© 1971 by Suzanne Best. The Stephen Greene Press

Baked Haddock
four servings

4 pieces **haddock fillet**, serving size (other white fish can be used)

bread stuffing	**fish sauce**
1 1/2 cups of day-old bread	4 tbsp of butter
1/2 cup of chopped green onion	2 tbsp of finely chopped onion
1/2 cup of chopped celery	1 clove, fresh garlic, crushed, chopped
1/4 cup of chopped red bell pepper	1 tbsp of anchovy paste/2 fillets minced
8 small mushrooms cut in half	1 tbsp of capers *(Optional)*
(optional) 2/3 cups chopped ham or oysters	1 tsp of Worcestershire sauce

Pre heat oven to 350°. Grease a baking dish big enough for haddock.

Bread stuffing: Put the bread, gently pulled into bite-sized pieces, into a bowl. In a pan, braise the chopped vegetables in a little butter and either stock or water until soft. Without compacting the bread, toss in the vegetables. *(Optional)* Toss in the ham or drained oysters. *(Optional)* Add 1/2 cup chopped spinach or kale and a little fresh tarragon, dill, or fennel to taste. Put the stuffing in the bottom of the baking dish and lay the fish fillets on top.

Bake just until the fish flakes when touched, about 25 minutes. In the vegatable pan, make the sauce: Melt the butter and gently cook the onion and garlic until soft. Add the anchovy paste, capers, and Worcestershire sauce. Serve stuffed fish on a plate. Spoon sauce over fish. Dust with a small amount of grated Parmesan or Romano cheese. Garnish with a lemon wedge.

Ratatouille Québécoise

ten servings

Restaurants in Old Quebec City

Ratatouille is originally a French dish from Nice. It is popular all over the French-speaking world, including Quebec. There are many variations.

3 cups diced eggplant	4 fresh poblano peppers, seeded, sliced thin
1/2 cup virgin olive oil	3 cups fresh Roma tomatoes, seeded, quartered
1 large red onion, sliced thin	3 cups fresh sliced summer squash/zucchini
3 cloves fresh garlic, sliced	2/3 cup pitted olives
1 inch fresh ginger, sliced	1/4 cup fresh roughly chopped basil
1/2 cup sliced crimini mushrooms	1/2 cup crème fraîche or sour cream
	salt, pepper, thyme

Dice and salt eggplant to draw moisture. When it is quite wet, drain and pat with paper towel to dry. Into a deep frying pan, add olive oil, onion, and garlic; sauté lightly. Add eggplant, ginger, mushrooms, peppers, tomatoes, summer squash, and olives, and toss. Cover and simmer for 45 minutes, (low heat). Uncover and cook longer to reduce liquid, 15 or 20 minutes. Add salt, a pinch of thyme, and a liberal grinding of black pepper. Garnish with fresh basil and dollops of crème fraîche. Serve toasted rounds of a fresh baguette, and a side salad of torn-up Romaine lettuce, toasted sliced almonds, and mandarin orange sections with an oil and vinegar dressing.

Apple Delights

by Beatrice Vaughan of Thetford, Vermont

Paper-Bag Apple Pie

Preheat oven to 425°.

6 to 7 cups peeled, sliced apples	unbaked 9-inch pie shell
1/2 cup maple syrup, 1/2 cup sugar	2 tbsp lemon juice
1/2 cup flour + 2 tbsp	1/2 tsp grated lemon rind (zest)
1/2 tsp ground nutmeg	1 stick (1/2 cup) softened butter

Combine apple slices, 1/2 cup of maple syrup (or brown sugar if maple isn't available), and 2 tbsp flour. Add nutmeg (and cinnamon, optional) and toss well to mix. Turn into the pie shell and sprinkle with lemon juice. Combine 1/2 cup of sugar with 1/2 cup of flour, rub in the butter with a spoon, and sprinkle the topping evenly over the apples. Place the pie in a large, heavy paper bag. Fold the end over twice and fasten with paper clips. Place the bag on a cookie sheet. Bake in 425° oven for 1 hour. Split bag open and remove the pie to cool. Serve cool with good cheddar cheese.

This is a delectable pie. The apples will be very tender, the top golden. And somehow the paper bag ensures a perfect bake every time.

Old-Time Vermont Curried Lamb

1 tsp or more curry powder	2 tbsp flour
3 tbsp butter, melted	1 cup chicken or mushroom broth
1 medium onion, peeled and sliced	1 tbsp lemon juice
1 large stalk celery, trimmed and sliced	salt, if needed, and fresh ground pepper
8 small mushrooms, trimmed and sliced	1/2 tsp cumin seeds (optional)
2 medium apples, peeled and sliced	3 tbsp candied ginger, diced (optional)
2 cups diced cooked lamb with drippings	cooked rice for four servings

Add curry powder and cumin to melted butter in heavy frying pan, then onions, celery, and apples. Simmer until onion is tender. With strainer spoon, remove vegetables and apple. In the same pan, brown the lamb; remove with strainer spoon. Blend flour into the fat in the pan, then stir in the broth and bring to boiling, stirring constantly. Return vegetables, apples, and lamb to pan. Stir in lemon juice. Add salt, if needed, some fresh ground pepper, and candied ginger. Serve hot with rice. Garnish with raisins or dried cranberries, shredded coconut, and chutney.

Glazed Apples for Ham. Core unpeeled apples and slice in thick rings. Boil together 1 cup light brown sugar (or 1 cup maple syrup), the juice of one orange, and 2 tbsp of butter until syrup is fairly thick. Add apple rings and simmer until tender and glazed. Serve with ham.

My grandfather used to say, "never trust a lean cook."

Recipes from Bea Vaughan's Apple Cooking *and* The Old Cook's Almanac
Copyright © 1966, 1969 by Beatrice Vaughan. The Stephen Greene Press.

THE BACKSIDE CAFÉ

24 HIGH STREET
BRATTLEBORO, VERMONT
05301

802.257.5056

BREAKFAST

TAKE-AWAY MENU

Monday-Saturday
7:00 AM - 8:00 PM

backsidecafe@gmail.com
Check us out on Facebook!

**SCRAMBLES ~ PANCAKES
BREAKFAST SANDWICHES & WRAPS
~ MOCHA JOES LOCAL COFFEE ~**

QUICK BITES

To-go wraps & breakfast sandwiches designed to be simple and faster than entrees, served without sides or extras!

EGG SANDWICHES
SERVED ON AN ENGLISH MUFFIN

BACON, EGG & CHEESE fried egg, bacon & cheddar	3.99
HAM, EGG & CHEESE fried egg, ham & cheddar	3.99
SAUSAGE, EGG & CHEESE fried egg, sausage patties & cheddar	3.99
AVOCADO, EGG & CHEESE fried egg, avocado & cheddar	3.99

ADD MEAT or AVOCADO	2.00
ADD AMERICAN, SWISS, CHEDDAR	1.00
ADD TOMATO or RED ONION	.50
ON BAGEL	.75
ON SPECIALTY THICK ARTISAN BREAD	2.00

BREAKFAST WRAPS
SERVED IN A WARM 12" FLOUR TORTILLA

EGG & CHEESE scrambled eggs & melted cheddar	4.99
BACON, EGG & CHEESE scrambled eggs, bacon & melted cheddar	5.99
HAM, EGG & CHEESE scrambled eggs, ham & melted cheddar	5.99
SAUSAGE, EGG & CHEESE scrambled eggs, sausage & melted cheese	5.99
GREEN GODDESS WRAP scrambled eggs, baby spinach, avocado, homemade pesto & melted cheddar !!	6.99

CAFE SCRAMBLES

Three-egg scrambles served with toast & homefried potatoes

SIMPLE SCRAMBLE	5.99
just three eggs scrambled	
VT CHEDDAR SCRAMBLE	6.99
scrambled eggs with melted cheddar	
HAM & CHEDDAR SCRAMBLE	8.99
eggs, smoked ham & melted cheddar	
BACON & CHEDDAR SCRAMBLE	8.99
eggs, bacon & melted cheddar	
SAUSAGE & CHEDDAR SCRAMBLE	8.99
eggs, breakfast sausage & cheddar	
AVOCADO & CHEDDAR SCRAMBLE	8.99
eggs, fresh avocado & melted cheddar	
BACKSIDE SCRAMBLE	7.99
eggs, melted Vermont cheddar cheese, fresh garlic, mushrooms & onions	
SPINACH SCRAMBLE	7.99
eggs, baby spinach, fresh garlic, tomatoes & melted Vermont cheddar cheese	
SPANISH SCRAMBLE	7.99
eggs, onions, green peppers, homemade salsa, fresh tomatoes & melted cheddar	
WESTERN SCRAMBLE	7.99
eggs, onions, peppers & smoked ham	

ADD TO BUILD YOUR OWN SCRAMBLE:

Cheddar, American, Swiss	1.00
Provolone, Sharp Cheddar, Feta	1.50
Bacon, Ham, Sausage	2.00
Fresh Avocado	2.00
Baby Spinach	1.00
Homemade Pesto	1.50
Onion, Pepper or Mushroom	.50
Fresh Garlic or Tomato	.50
Egg Beaters	1.50
Extra Egg	1.00

FROM THE GRIDDLE

Served with butter & table syrup - Vermont Maple available for 2.00

FULL STACK PANCAKES (3)	6.99
SHORT STACK PANCAKES (2)	5.00
FRENCH TOAST	5.99
made with two slices thick sourdough	
FRESH FRUIT TOPPING	add 2.50

BREAKFAST SIDES

MIXED GREENS	3.00
HOMEMADE SALSA	1.00
SOUR CREAM	.75
HALF AVOCADO	3.00
BACON	3.00
HAM	3.00
SAUSAGE PATTIES	3.00
HOMEFRIES	3.00
PEANUT BUTTER	.75
CREAM CHEESE	.75
BAGEL	2.50
BAGEL with CREAM CHEESE	3.00
ENGLISH MUFFIN	2.00

WHEN ORDERING
BREAKFAST ENTREES,
YOU MAY REPLACE ANY SIDE OF
TOAST OR
HOMEFRIED POTATOES
WITH A SIDE OF MIXED GREENS FOR
AN ADDITIONAL $1.50

Consuming raw or undercooked meats, poultry, seafood, shellfish or eggs may increase your risk of food-borne illness, especially if you have certain medical conditions

Welcome to

SUNDAY BRUNCH AT THE MARINA 10-1

BRUNCH BUFFET...............$15

ALL YOU CAN EAT BUFFET,

SALADS, PASTRIES AND DESSERTS

ADD AN OMELET *for an extra* $2.00 *ask your server*

(OMELETS AVAILABLE UNTIL 12 ONLY)

FROM THE KITCHEN

EGGS BENEDICT........$10

TWO POACHED EGGS WITH CANADIAN BACON

ON AN ENGLISH MUFFIN SMOTHERED IN

HOLLANDAISE SAUCE SERVED WITH HOMEFRIES

HUEVOS RANCHEROS....$10

FRIED EGG ON A FLOUR TORTILLA WITH REFRIED BEANS,

SALSA, AND MELTED CHEESE SERVED WITH HOMEFRIES

FULL MARINA MENU AVAILABLE ALL DAY

FROM THE BAR

MARINA MARY

TWO GRILLED SHRIMP, ONE PIECIE OF APPLEWOOD SMOKED BACON AND MARINA'S

OWN BLOODY MARY MIX WITH VODKA AND AN OLIVE GARNISH *IT'S A MEAL IN ITSELF* 12

HOT AND SPICY MARTINI

VODKA, A SPLASH OF PEPPERONCINI AND OLIVE JUICE WITH A SPLASH OF BLOODY MARY MIX

SHAKEN UNTIL CHILLED TO PERFECTION SERVED WITH A PEPPERONCIN OLIVE GARNISH 10

BLOODY MARY

WITH CELERY AND OLIVE GARNISH 7.50

MIMOSA

WINE GLASS FILLED WITH CHAMPAGNE AND ICE WITH A SPLASH OF OJ 7

CHAMPAGNE BY THE BOTTLE

CHANDON CHAMPAGNE SPLITS 16

KORBEL BRUT CHAMPAGNE 22

CAVIT LUNETTA PROSECCO ITALIAN SPARKLING WINE 28

Amy's *Bakery Arts* Cafe

Lunch served 11am - 5pm

FRESH SOUP served w/ today's fresh bread....cup $4.25 bowl...$5.25

SALADS
made with organic mixed greens; fresh bread and salad dressing on the side

Mixed Green Salad: choose bleu cheese, green goddess, champagne or balsamic vinaigrette $4.75

Greek Salad: feta cheese, onion, olives, cherry tomatoes, cucumbers w/ champagne vinaigrette $9.00

Fresh Mozzarella Salad: basil pesto, oven-roasted romas & olives w/ balsamic vinaigrette $10.00

Cobb Salad: natural chicken breast, cherry tomatoes, avocado, egg & bacon, w/ bleu cheese dressing $12.00

VT Goat Cheese Salad: candied walnuts, fig-olive tapenade, cherry tomatoes, balsamic syrup & balsamic vinaigrette $12.00

Half Avocado Salad: avocado half filled with your choice of dilly chicken salad , lemony tuna salad, or hummus w/ a mixed green salad and your choice of dressing (bleu cheese, champagne or balsamic vinaigrette, green goddess) $11.00

HOT SANDWICHES

Rockin' Reuben: house-braised corned beef, swiss, sauerkraut, special sauce on country sourdough $9.00

Tempeh Reuben: the vegetarian classic on organic multigrain sourdough. Go vegan with avocado and maple mustard! $8.50

Black Forest Ham and Swiss: caramelized apples and onions, maple mustard on country sourdough $7.75

Molten Mozzarella: fresh mozzarella, basil pesto & oven-roasted romas on baguette $7.75

Tasty Tuna Melt: lemony tuna salad (dolphin-safe), VT cheddar, avocado and tomato on country sourdough $8.25

Garlicky Chicken: hormone-free chicken breast, feta-garlic spread, fig-olive tapenade, tomato on country sourdough $7.75

COLD SANDWICHES

Chicken Dagwood: hormone-free chicken breast, cranberry chutney, natural bacon, Vermont cheddar, avocado, lettuce, tomato, mayo, maple mustard on country sourdough $9.00

California BLT: natural bacon, avocado, lettuce and tomato w/ mayo on country sourdough $7.75

Dilly Chicken Salad: hormone-free chicken, creamy dill dressing, lettuce, tomato on country sourdough $7.75

Hummus Deluxe: house-made hummus, avocado, feta-garlic spread, cucumbers, carrots, lettuce, sprouts, tomato on organic multigrain sourdough $7.25

Very Veggie: avocado, sprouts, carrots, cucumbers, lettuce, tomato & mayo on organic multigrain sourdough $6.25

113 Main Street Brattleboro VT 05301   802 251-1071

Lunch & Dinner

Chelsea Royal Favorites

Appetizers & Sides

Super Nachos With cheese, tomatoes, jalapeños, sour cream, olives, shredded lettuce and salsa ranchero ›› 7.99

Buffalo Wings Brattleboro's Best ›› 7.50

Potato Skins With cheddar, bacon, scallions and sour cream ›› 6.99

Garlic Bread ›› 3.50

Soup Cup ›› 2.99 Bowl ›› 3.75

Tossed Salad ›› 4.50

French Fries ›› 3.50

Sweet Potato Fries ›› 4.25

Onion Rings ›› 4.99

Macaroni & Cheese ›› 4.75

Coleslaw or Pasta Salad ›› 2.99

Baked Beans ›› 3.99

Vermont Cabot Cottage Cheese ›› 2.50

Pizzas (10 inch)

Greek Feta, red onion, spinach, garlic and kalamata olives ›› 10.50

Meat Lovers Pepperoni, bacon, ham, sausage and meatballs ›› 10.50

White Pesto Lovers Ricotta cheese, our own basil pesto, sliced tomatoes, spinach and kalamata olives ›› 10.50

The BBQ Grilled chicken, red onion, cilantro and Royal BBQ sauce ›› 10.50

Personal Pizza (10 inch) ›› 6.00 additional toppings ›› 0.85 each

Choice of bacon, sausage, pepperoni, anchovies, meatballs, feta cheese, broccoli, mushrooms, onion, spinach, diced tomatoes, fresh garlic, black olives and green peppers

Burgers & Sandwiches

Served with Chips & Pickle (Unless Noted Otherwise)
Upgrade to French Fries ›› 2.00 Sweet Potato Fries ›› 3.00

Footlong Hotdog ›› 4.25

Grilled Cheese ›› 3.99

Burger 6 oz. Made with local grass-fed ground beef ›› 5.50 With cheese ›› 5.99

Bacon & Mushroom Burger Made with local grass-fed ground beef ›› 6.25

Blue Cheese & Canadian Bacon Burger Made with local grass-fed ground beef ›› 6.99

100% Bison Cheddar Burger Made with local pasture-raised bison ›› 7.99

Veggie Burger ›› 5.99

Philly Cheese Steak Made with local grass-fed beef and served with french fries ›› 8.99

Steak Sandwich Made with local grass-fed beef and served with french fries ›› 9.99

Buffalo Chicken Sandwich With blue cheese dressing ›› 7.99

Grilled Maple BBQ Chicken Sandwich Served on a bulky roll ›› 6.99

Reuben Thinly sliced corned beef with Swiss cheese, sauerkraut and Russian dressing on grilled rye ›› 6.99

Teriyaki Chicken Club ›› 7.50

Roast Beef, Turkey, or Ham & Cheese ›› 5.99

Turkey Club ›› 6.99

Tuna Salad ›› 5.99 **Tuna Melt** ›› 6.50

B.L.T. ›› 4.50

Meatloaf Sandwich Grilled on a sub roll with cranberry sauce and Swiss cheese. Served with mashed potatoes and gravy ›› 6.99

Fishwich Lightly battered haddock with classic American cheese, our own tartar sauce on a toasted bun, with lettuce and tomato on the side ›› 5.99

Clam Roll Served with french fries and coleslaw ›› 8.99

Platters

Hot Open-Faced Roast Beef or Turkey Sandwich With choice of potato and vegetable ›› 8.99

Macaroni & Cheese with Footlong Hotdog Made with Vermont cheddar cheese ›› 6.99

Spaghetti Marinara & Garlic Bread ›› 7.50 With meatballs ›› 8.99

Grilled Liver & Onions With bacon and a choice of potato and vegetable ›› 9.99

BBQ Pulled Pork Sandwich Smoked here, with our own Royal BBQ sauce. Served with baked beans and coleslaw ›› 8.99

Fresh Baked or Fried Haddock With lemon butter, choice of potato and vegetable ›› 9.99

Rotisserie 1/2 Chicken BBQ or traditional with choice of potato and vegetable ›› 9.99

Boneless Pork Chops Breaded and fried, served with gravy, applesauce, and choice of potato and vegetable ›› 9.99

Buffalo Bill's Feast 100% Natural Buffalo: One grilled buffalo dog, and one 6 oz. bison burger served with sweet potato fries and coleslaw ›› 11.99

Chicken or Eggplant Parmesan With spaghetti and garlic bread ›› 10.99

Veal Parmesan With spaghetti and garlic bread ›› 12.99

Mom's Meatloaf With a choice of potato, vegetable and gravy ›› 9.50

Meat Lasagna With garlic bread ›› 8.99

Vegetable Lasagna Zucchini, broccoli, peppers, mushrooms, marinara sauce, and garlic bread ›› 8.99

Roast Loin of Pork With stuffing, apple sauce and choice of potato and vegetable ›› 9.99

Fisherman's Platter Fried shrimp, scallops and haddock served with french fries and coleslaw ›› 14.99

Fried Scallops With french fries and coleslaw ›› 14.99

Roast Turkey & Stuffing With cranberry sauce and choice of potato, and vegetable ›› 9.99

Teriyaki Chicken Breast With choice of potato and vegetable ›› 9.99

Char-Grilled Grass-Fed Rib Eye Steak Locally raised, with choice of potato and vegetable. King Cut ›› 15.99 Queen Cut ›› 13.99

Salads

Chef Salad Turkey, ham, Swiss and cheddar cheese, with tomatoes, olives, cucumbers, and a hard boiled egg ›› 7.50

Caesar Salad ›› 5.99 (side Caesar ›› 4.99) Add grilled chicken breast ›› 7.99 Grilled shrimp or tenderloin ›› 11.99

Great Greek Salad Feta cheese, green peppers, onions, kalamata olives, tomatoes, cucumbers, and pepperoncini ›› 7.99

Spinach Salad Mushrooms, feta cheese, boiled egg, black olives, croutons, bacon, onions and tomatoes ›› 7.99

Our Own Dressings Creamy Dill, Blue Cheese, Russian, Italian, Ranch, Greek, Maple Balsamic Vinaigrette, Fat-Free Roasted Garlic Vinaigrette

Did you know?

All of our veal, steaks, burgers, ground beef, and grilled liver are from *local*, grass-fed beef.

Our seafood is New England's *finest* and delivered to us fresh.

Whenever possible, we use *hand-picked* seasonal vegetables from our own garden.

Having breakfast? Try our own *farm fresh* eggs!

SHIN LA RESTAURANT

57 Main St. 802.257.5226
WWW.SHINLARESTAURANT.COM
Monday – Thursday 11:00 – 9:00
Friday – Saturday 11:00 – 9:30

APPETIZERS

Shumai (6) 6.25
Choose steamed OR deep fried shrimp dumplings
Yakimandoo (5) 6.25
Pan-fried pork OR vegetarian tofu dumplings
Yakitori (2)..6.25
Deep fried teriyaki chicken & vegetables on a stick
Kara Age 6.25
Deep fried tempura chicken w/ teriyaki sauce
Age Tofu 6.25
Deep fried tofu w/ ginger dipping sauce
Teriyaki Tofu 6.25
Deep fried tofu w/ teriyaki sauce
Tempura 8.95
Deep fried jumbo shrimp & vegetables
Steamed Tofu 6.25
Tofu w/ sweet soy sauce and spices
Edamame 6.25
Boiled young soybean pods sprinkled with salt
Eggroll (2) 4.95

SIDES

Kimchi 4.25
Spicy fermented napa cabbage
Seaweed Salad 6.25
Choose sweet OR spicy
Cucumber Salad 4.25
Spinach Salad 4.50
Rice..2.25

SOUPS

Chicken & Rice 3.95/4.25
Miso 3.95/4.25
Hot Noodle 7.50
Add tofu, spinach, egg, or kimchi .75 each
New Year 7.95
Fish base w/ sliced rice cake, egg & scallions
Yook Gae Jang 10.95
Spicy soup w/ shredded beef, egg, glass noodles, scallions & rice
Soon Doo Boo Chigae 10.95
Spicy stew w/ silken tofu, vegetables, seafood & a side of rice
Deon Jang Chigae 10.95
Spicy bean paste stew w/tofu, vegetable, seafood & a side of rice

SOUPS

Udon 10.95
Fish base soup w/thick noodles & assorted vegetables & seafood
Tempura Udon 13.95
Udon w/ two jumbo tempura shrimp
Nabeyaki Udon 14.95
Udon w/ two jumbo tempura shrimp, chicken, and egg

KOREAN

Shumai (12) 10.95
Steamed shrimp dumplings with sauce
Yakimandoo (10) 10.95
Pan-fried pork OR vegetarian tofu dumplings
Bool Go Ki 15.95/19.95
Sliced marinated beef with sides of rice, kimchi & cucumber salad
Gopdol Bi Bim Bap 12.95
Sautéed vegetables over rice in hot stone bowl. Add egg or tofu .75
Bi Bim Bap 10.95
Marinated oriental vegetables over rice. Add egg or tofu .75
Jap Chae Bap 10.95
Sautéed sweet potato glass noodles w/mixed vegetables over rice
Noodle Salad 10.95
Cold wheat noodles w/sliced egg, cucumber, turkey & crab
Bokeumbap 10.95/13.95
Vegetable OR shrimp fried rice & salad
Hae Mul Pa Chun..................................15.95
Seafood scallion pancake w/savory dipping sauce
Ohjingau Bokeum..................................15.95
Sautéed squid w/ vegetables in a spicy sauce & a side of rice
Tangsuyuk...15.95
Sweet & sour tempura chicken w/vegetables & a side of rice

JAPANESE

Chicken Teriyaki....................................15.95
Grilled teriyaki chicken w/ steamed vegetables & a side of rice
Beef Teriyaki 15.95
Grilled teriyaki beef w/ steamed vegetables & a side of rice
Salmon Teriyaki....................................16.95
Grilled teriyaki salmon w/ steamed vegetables & a side of rice
Yasai Dame...10.95
Stir-fried vegetables & a side of rice
Vegetable Tempura 14.95
Deep-fried tempura vegetables
Shrimp Tempura 17.95
Deep-fried jumbo tempura shrimp and vegetables
Ton Katsu 13.95
Breaded pork cutlet & a side of rice
Chicken Katsu 13.95
Breaded chicken cutlet & a side of rice
Fish Katsu 15.95
Breaded fish cutlet & a side of rice
Katsu Donburi......................................13.95
Breaded deep fried chicken simmered w/sauce, egg, peppers over rice
Tempura Donburi...................................13.95
Jumbo tempura shrimp & vegetables w/sauce over rice.
Yaki Soba..12.95
Stir-fry noodles w/ vegetables. Choice of chicken, beef, or tofu

PLEASE SEE SEPARATE MENU FOR SUSHI

Tulip

Café Hours

7:00 am – 5:00 pm
Monday – Friday
9:00 am – 5:00 pm
Saturday & Sunday
Kitchen closes at 4:00 pm

12 Harmony Place
Brattleboro, Vermont
(802) 490.2061

Hot Buffet Specials

Crepes

Savory –(Gluten Free Buckwheat Batter)

Served with your choice of Bulgur or Shredded Vegetable salad. (Bulgur contains gluten)

• **Spinach & Feta**- *Spinach with caramelized onion & Turkish feta.* - **$7.50**

• **Breakfast Galette**- *Ham, Egg & Cheddar Cheese* - **$7.50**

• **Veggie Crepe**- *Roasted Zucchini, Red Pepper, Mushroom, Baby Spinach & Feta* - **$8.99**

• **Kavurma**-*Turkish style spicy ground beef with cheddar cheese, tomatoes, peppers, and onions. Add egg $0.50* - **$7.99**

Salads

• **Grilled Chicken**- *Grilled chicken breast, walnuts, Dried cranberries, red onion, feta cheese, organic spring mix with pomegranate vinaigrette*- **$ 7.99**

• **Mediterranean**- *Olives, fresh mozzarella, Red Onion, Cherry Tomato, Roasted Red Peppers, organic spring mix with pomegranate vinaigrette*- **$7.50**

•**Half avocado**– *Sliced avocado, radish, snow peas, tomatoes, red onions, feta cheese, organic spring mix with lemon vinaigrette*- **$8:99**

•**Kisir**- *Mixed greens with bulgur (celery, cabbage, onion, pepper paste and hard-boiled egg*- **$7.50**

•**Sassy Mushroom**- *Portobello mushroom, caramelized onions, green beans, toasted almonds, green apple, mixed greens & pomegranate dressing* - **$8.99**

Smoothies
(seasonal)

Soup
(seasonal)

Ice Cream
(seasonal)

Cold Sandwiches

*Served on Turkish Pide bread with chips & a pickle.

• **BLT**- Bacon, Lettuce, Tomato, and Mayo - **$6.99**

• **Mama Noor's Humus**– *Homemade Humus, Olive Paste, Tomatoes, Avocado & Greens.* - **$ 7.99**

• **Caprese**-*Fresh mozzarella, tomato, pesto* - **$7.25**

• **Turkey Brie**- *Turkey, Brie Cheese, Dijon Walnut Mayo& Green Apple* - **$ 7.99**

Panini

*Served on Your Choice of Multigrain or White Bread with chips & a pickle.

• **Turkey Chipotle**- *Turkey, Chipotle aioli, caramelized onions, banana peppers & Provolone* - **$8.99**

• **The Balkan**- *Grilled Chicken, Baby Spinach, Bosnian Ajvar paste (mix veggie spread) & Provolone* - **$7.99**

• **Garden Panini**- *Roasted Red Pepper, Mushroom, Zucchini, Pesto, Spinach Leaves & Feta* - **$7.99**

• **Turkey Pesto**- *Turkey, Pesto, Sun Dried Tomato w/ Fresh Mozzarella* - **$7.99**

• **Italian**- *Ham, mortadella & tuscano salami with provolone, roasted tomatoes and mustard*- **$8.99**

• **3 Cheese**- *Mozzarella, Provolone & Feta with pesto and baby spinach*- **$7.50**

• **Chicken&Avocado**- *Sliced avocado, grilled chicken, pepper jack cheese and onions*- **$7.99**

SpecialtyEspresso

Café Aulait
Small- $2.55..........................Large- $2.85
Americano
Single-$2.05..........................Double- $2.55
Macchiato
Single-$2.27..........................Double- $2.77
Breve
Single-$3.45..........................Double- $3.95
Latte
Single- $2.95..........................Double- $3.45
Cappuccino
Single- $2.73..........................Double- $3.32
Espresso
Single- $2.05..........................Double- $2.55
Mocha Latte
Single- $3.23..........................Double- $3.73
Mochacino
Single-$2.99..........................Double- $3.45
Local Chai Latte
Small- $3.00..........................Large- $3.50
Hot Chocolate
Small-$2.68..........................Large- $3.14
Steamer (With any flavor shot)
Small-$2.23..........................Large- $2.75

*Add an Extra Shot of Espresso for $0.75

Flavor Shots- *Vanilla, Carmel, Hazelnut, Chocolate, Maple, Raspberry, Peach, Coconut, or Spices*
Add- ¢50 – **Add to any Specialty Drink**
*Tax not included in Specialty drink prices.

TOP of the HILL GRILL

EAT IN • TAKE OUT • CATERING
OUTDOOR PATIO • INDOOR DECKHOUSE

(802) 258-9178

632 Putney Road
Brattleboro, VT 05301
www.topofthehillgrill.com
topofthehillgrill@ymail.com

B-B-Q PLATES

Beef Burnt Ends	$12.95
Combo Plate – ¼ Chicken, Beef Brisket, Pulled Pork Or Rib	$18.95
Half Grilled Chicken	$11.95
Apple Smoked Turkey	$11.95
Hickory Smoked Pulled Pork	$13.95
Hickory Smoked Beef Brisket	$12.95
Hickory Smoked Ribs.half Rack	$15.95
Full Rack	$28.95

All plates include coleslaw, cornbread, baked beans, sauce

SANDWICHES

HOT DOG	$2.95
SLOPPY JOE	$3.95
TEMPEH BURGER – *w/lettuce, tomato, onion*	$6.95
GRILLED CHICKEN BREAST	$7.95
SMOKED TURKEY BREAST	$7.95
SMOKED PULLED PORK	$8.95
SMOKED BEEF BRISKET	$7.95
CAJUN CATFISH – *w/chipotle lime sauce*	$8.95
SAUSAGE – *choice of sausage w/grilled P's & O's*	$7.95
HAMBURGER – *w/lettuce, tomato, onion*	$7.95
CHEESEBURGER – *lettuce, tomato, onion, and swiss or cheddar*	$8.50
PATTY MELT BURGER – *w/caramelized onions, swiss or cheddar, rye bread*	$7.95

TORTILLA ROLL UPS

*On your choice of plain, whole wheat, garlic-herb,
sun-dried tomato or jalapeno-cheddar tortilla*

SMOKED PULLED PORK	$8.95
SMOKED BEEF BRISKET	$7.95
SMOKED TURKEY	$7.95
GRILLED CHICKEN	$7.95
TEMPEH – *w/pepper's & onions*	$7.95
COMBO-WRAPS – *your choice of ingredients*	$8.95

"OUR OWN" SAUSAGE

Ground, seasoned, filled and smoked here at Top of the Hill Grill
PORK - Spicy Andouille or Savory Smoked
CHICKEN - Spicy Jamaican Jerk or Savory Smoked

SAUSAGE SANDWICH – *w/peppers & onions on a crusty roll*	$8.95
SAUSAGE ON A BED OF GREENS	$7.95
SAUSAGE & COLLARDS – *includes cornbread*	$9.95

SLIDERS

JERK CHICKEN- *with Island Fire Sauce*......................$3.50
ANDOUILLE *with blue cheese, pickle, and spicy mustard*..................$3.50
LAMB- *with cumin/corriander and red onion* $3.50
PULLED PORK- *with BBQ Sauce and pickle*.......................$4.00

HOUSE SPECIALS

YO MAMA'S UMAMI BURGER
"The 5th Taste" with porcini powder and shaved parmesan..............$7.95
STEVE-O WRAP $7.95
Rice, cheese, greens, black beans, tomatoes, slaw, chipotle-lime sauce
HEIDI'S SPECIAL WRAP $7.95
Grilled tempeh, P's & O's, potatoes, cheese, slaw, BBQ sauce
SHADER SPECIAL....................................$8.95
Cheeseburger, sautéed P's & O's, fajita seasonings, ranch dressing
PAGINATOR $7.95
Chicken breast, cheddar, guacamole, bacon, lettuce, tomato on a bun
NIKKI'S WRAP $7.95
Chicken, cheese, P's & O's, potatoes, mustard sauce
KELSEY'S CATFISH WRAP....................................$8.95
Cajun catfish, sautéed P's & O's, tomato, chipotle-lime sauce
PATTY MELT $7.95
Thin burger, caramelized onions, swiss or cheddar, grilled rye bread
BEEF BURNT ENDS – *Pile, Wrap or Sandwich* $9.95
TURKEY REUBEN $7.95
Smoked turkey, Russian dressing, swiss, sauerkraut, grilled rye bread

---

VEGETARIAN or MEAT FREE

Rice dishes contain chicken broth

BURRITO – *refried beans, rice, lettuce, cheese, salsa, sour cream*....$7.95
TEMPEH – *Wrap $7.95 • Burrito $8.95 • Burger $6.50 • Over greens* $7.95
ROASTED ROOT VEGETABLES $3.95
ROASTED GARLIC POTATOES....................................$3.50
TWICE BAKED POTATOES.........................$3.95
MAC-N-CHEESE.........................$7.95
BLACK BEANS & RICE* - *w/cheese & salsa*.........................$3.95
CAJUN RICE* $3.50
RED BEANS & RICE*- *includes cornbread*.........................$7.95
CHEESE QUESADILLA – *includes salsa & sour cream*..................$7.25
BED OF GREENS SALAD – *w/Italian, Balsamic or Ranch dressing*......$3.95
BILL'S PLATE.........................$7.95
Mesclun greens, potato salad, Cajun rice, coleslaw, roasted root vegetables*
GRILLED PORTOBELLO.........................$7.95
with "the works" and garlic aoli

CAJUN

CHICKEN & SAUSAGE GUMBO - *with cornbread*..................$7.95
GRILLED CATFISH
with a side of chipotle-lime sauce served over Cajun rice $9.25
served on a bun w/lettuce and tomato $8.95
JAMBALAYA - *includes cornbread.* $8.95
CAJUN RICE..................$3.50
RED BEANS & RICE - *includes cornbread.* $7.95
ADD - chicken or sausage..................$9.95

MEXICAN

TACOS – *2 fish or chicken tacos in corn tortillas w/black beans/rice* ...$8.95
FAJITAS – *chicken, beef, pork or turkey*..................$9.50
Includes grilled peppers & onions, salsa, sour cream, tortillas
QUESADILLA – *includes salsa and sour cream*
Cheese..................$7.25
Chicken, beef, pork, or tempeh..................$8.95
CHILI – *includes cornbread* – CUP..........$3.95   BOWL $7.25
BURRITOS – *Refried beans, rice, lettuce, cheese, salsa, sour cream* $7.95
Add chicken, beef, pork, turkey or tempeh..................$8.95
ENCHILADA – *Chicken or pork, served with black beans and rice*......$9.95
BLACK BEANS & RICE – *w/cheese & salsa* $3.95

HOMEMADE SIDES & SALADS

COLLARD GREENS – *w/roasted tomatoes & bacon* $2.95
BED OF SALAD GREENS – *Italian, Balsamic or Ranch dressing* $3.95
– ADD –
sausage, chicken, turkey, beef brisket, pulled pork or tempeh..............$7.95

POTATO SALAD..................$2.95
CORNBREAD..................$ .95
COLESLAW..................$2.50
BAKED BEANS $1.95
TWICE BAKED POTATOES..................$3.95
ROASTED ROOT VEGETABLES $3.95
ROASTED GARLIC-ROSEMARY POTATOES $3.50
CAJUN RICE..................$3.50
BLACK BEANS & RICE – *w/cheese & salsa* $3.95
MAC-N-CHEESE – *made with Grafton cheddar*..................$7.95

NOTICE: Consuming raw or undercooked meats, poultry, seafood, shellfish, or eggs may increase your risk of foodborne illness.

THE SUNDRIED TOMATO
Taste the Mediterranean

Wine and Beer Available!

1300 Putney Road
Brattleboro, VT 05301
802-251-0010

MasterCard VISA

Appetizers

Buffalo Hot Wings (10 pcs) 6.99
Chicken Fingers (6pcs) 6.49
Mozzarella Stix (8 pcs) 6.49
Jalapeno Poppers (8 pcs) 6.49
Basket of Fries 3.75
Cajun Curly Fries 4.49
Onion Rings 4.49
Cheese Fries 5.49
Chicken Fingers & Fries 7.49
Stuffed Grape Leaves (12 pcs) 6.49
Garlic Bread ....1.99 w/cheese 2.50

Salads
Dressing Choices
Greek - Ranch - Blue Cheese
Fat free Italian

* Additional Salad dressing will cost Extra	Small	Large
Garden Salad	5.49	5.99
Garden Salad w/ Mozzarella	5.99	6.49
Garden Salad w/Grilled Chicken	7.49	7.99
Garden Salad w/Tuna	5.99	6.49
Garden Salad w/Turkey	5.99	6.49
Greek	5.99	6.49
Antipasto		7.49

Pizza & Calzone

	Sm.	Lg.	Calzone
Cheese	7.99	10.49	7.99
One Topping	8.50	11.49	8.99
Two Topping	9.50	12.49	9.49
Three Topping	9.99	13.49	10.99
Four Topping	10.49	14.49	11.99
House Special	12.99	15.99	13.49
Meat Lovers	12.99	15.99	13.49
Mediterranean	12.99	15.99	13.49
Vegetarian	12.99	15.99	13.49

Toppings/Fillings

Mushroom - Onion - Green Pepper
Black Olives - Tomato - Garlic
Sundried Tomato - Spinach - Eggplant
Jalapeno - Broccoli - Steak - Salami
Meatball - Sausage - Pepperoni - Ham
Feta - Grilled Chicken - Gyro Meat

Burgers

	Reg.	Double
Hamburger	4.49	5.25
Cheese Burger	4.99	5.49
Bacon Cheese Burger	5.25	6.25

Deluxe Burgers

Comes with french fries or side salad

	Reg.	Double
Hamburger Deluxe	7.25	8.25
Cheese Burger Deluxe	7.75	8.75
Bacon Cheese Burger Deluxe	7.99	8.99

Mediterranean Plates

Gyro Plate	10.99
Chicken Plate	11.99
Combo Plate	12.99

Plates come with choice of fries or side salad

SMALL PLATES

Three Little Devils / deviled eggs with avocado & bacon filling 4
Track mix / peanuts, rice crackers, cashews, wasabi peas, spicy 3

Pub Chips / house made, rough cut **pub chips** with our addictive **Whetstoner Sauce** (sour cream, salsa, jalapenos, maple glazed bacon, blue cheese & assorted additional deliciousness) 6

Hummus Plate / lemon-artichoke hummus served with fresh cut veggies 8
Bean Dip / black bean & feta dip served with corn chips 5

SOUPS & SALADS

Cheddar Ale Soup / made with Grafton cheddar & Switchback ale 4
Whetstone Beef Chili / ground beef, seasoned pork, beans 6
Garten Plate / fresh greens, fresh vegetables, seasonal vinaigrette 7
Mediterranean Salad / salad blend, tomato, cucumber, onion, feta, tzatziki dressing 7

CHARCUTERIE

Vermont farmers market charcuterie board with three artisanal cheeses & two meats.
Great for sharing! Check out the chalkboard for todays local selections. 13

SANDWICHES & WRAPS

Greek Pita Pocket / hummus, feta, olive, onion, tomato, cucumber, tzatziki 8

The Bier Garten Brat / our traditionally made **German style Bratwurst** on a fresh **house baked roll** with seasoned **sauerkraut & our drunken mustard** 12

Buffalo Turkey Wrap / thin sliced turkey, blue cheese dressing, tomato, lettuce 11

All sandwiches served with our chefs selection of side

SODAS & DRINKS

Free refills on Coke, Diet Coke, Dr. Pepper,
Sprite, Orange Soda or Root Beer 2
a Bottle of Saratoga sparkling water 3
Iced Tea, Lemonade and juices 3

DESSERT & COFFEE

See today's dessert on the chalkboard

Locally Roasted Mocha Joes Coffee 2

Please place your order at the bar

Hungry for more? Enjoy our full restaurant downstairs.

WHETSTONE STATION CRAFT BEERS

NAME	NOTES FROM OUR BREWERS	ABV	IBU	$ / oz	4oz
Batch #62 Downtown Roasty Brown Brown Ale	As summer winds down, we welcome the coming fall with this well-balanced ale. Sweet and roasted malt flavors are balanced by the fragrance of Willamette and Simcoe hops. We hope you'll enjoy it as much as we do.	6%	28	$4.95 /16 oz	$1.80
Batch #66 Fall Harvest a Spiced Amber Ale	Ring in the harvest season with our spiced amber ale. This beer's slight sweetness is balanced with fresh ginger, split vanilla beans, cinnamon, and other festive spices, as well as a modest dose of Willamette hops in the boil.	6%	20	$4.95 /16 oz	$1.80
Batch #65 Whetstoner 1.0 a Pale Ale	Our Simarillo Pale Ale was such a big hit, we're bringing it back! Brewed slightly differently, but in the same spirit. This bright and delicious pale ale, brewed exclusively with Simcoe and Amarillo hops is big on aroma, with 6 pounds of hops added after flameout and dry hopped with another 4 pounds. Whetstoner is brewed just for you!	6%	40	$4.95 /12 oz	$2.25
Batch #63 The Baconator a smoked brown ale	Come with me if you want to live... This smoked, sweet, dark ale is something you have to experience. Brewed for the first annual Brattleboro Bacon Festival, we used the essence of our house maple smoked bacon to create this tasty treat. Served with a bacon garnish for a buck more.	6%	10	$4.95 /12 oz	$2.25

We are an "experimental nano-brewery", with a small (3.5 BBL) brewery and lab. We craft delicious beers about one hundred gallons at a time in unique styles or with unique methods (sometimes both!) documenting and sharing the process and recipes on our website.

Try a "flight"! 4oz pours of each of our house brewed craft beers for just $7

DINING ROOM DRAFT BEERS

NAME	FROM	STYLE	NOTES FROM OUR BEER GEEKS	ABV	IBU	$ / oz	4 oz
Victory - Headwater	PA	American Pale Ale	It's Hoppy... It's Victory.	5%	High	$4.95 /16 oz	$1.80
Northshire Equinox Pilsner	VT	Pilsner	Local (Bennington)-Classic Czech style pilsner	4%	Med	$5.40 /16 oz	$1.80
The Shed - Mountain Ale	VT	Brown Ale	A deliciously light but malty brown.	7%	Low	$5.40 /16 oz	$1.80
Ballast Point Sculpin	CA	American IPA	Currently the #1 rated IPA in the US!	7%	High	$6.30 /12 oz	$2.70
Green Flash Road Warrier	CA	Imperial Rye IPA	Crystal & rye malts dry-hopped w/ Mosaic	9%	80	$4.95 /8 oz	$2.70
Founders Oatmeal Stout	MI	Oatmeal Stout	Creamy, rich and delicous	5%	Low	$5.40 /16 oz	$1.80
Southern Tier Pumpking	NY	Vegetable Beer	Like drinking a glass of pumpkin pie	9%	Low	$4.50 /8 oz	$2.48
Liefmans Cuvee Brut	Belgium	Sour Red Ale	Tart, barrel aged with cherry's	6%	Low	$9.91 /8 oz	$5.40
Wurzburger Festbier	Germany	Oktoberfest/Marzen	A traditional Oktoberfest straight from Germany	6%	Low	$5.40 /16 oz	$1.80
Citizen Cider Unified Press	VT	Hard Cider	Dry, clean and crisp locally made cider	7%	N/A	$7.20 /12 oz	$2.93

NEW!! Make your own "flight" ! Pick up to five of the 4oz pours from above!

BOTTLES AND CANS

NAME	FROM	STYLE	NOTES FROM OUR BEER GEEKS	ABV	IBU	IN A	$
Czechvar	Czech Rep	Lager	This beer has been made for over 700 years	5%	23	11 oz Bottle	$3.60
Caldera Lawnmower Lager	OR	Lager	Low ABV sessionable lager	4%	Med	12 oz Can	$3.60
Long Trail Limbo	VT	IPA	A big, mouth-watering IPA	8%	80	12 oz Bottle	$4.95
Uinta Hop Nosh	UT	IPA	Bold and refreshing (formerly Hop Notch)	7%	82	12 oz Can	$4.95
Hopvalley Double D Blonde	OR	Blonde Ale	Easy going crisp and refreshing	5%	20	12 oz Can	$4.50
Founder's All Day IPA	MI	Session IPA	An IPA with Drinkablity, a true session beer.	5%	High	12 oz Can	$3.60
BBC Steel Rail	MA	Extra Pale Ale	What the water in heaven oughta taste like...	5%	20	12 oz Can	$4.50
Oakshire Overcast	OR	Espresso Stout	A silky oatmeal stout w/ espresso	6%	27	12 oz Can	$5.40
Finch's Brewing Fascist Pig	IL	Imperial Red Ale	Caramel & rye w/ a variety of hops	8%	Med	16 oz Can	$6.30
Rogue American Amber	CA	Amber Ale	Roasted malt accent, generous use of hops	5%	53	16 oz Can	$6.30
Einbecker Non Alcoholic	Germany	Non Alcoholic	A tasty non alcoholic German Beer	1%	Low	11 oz Bottle	$5.40
Green's Gluten Free Amber Ale	Belgium	Gluten Free Amber Ale	Organic, gluten free, cage free, tasty stuff!	6%	32	17 oz Bottle	$9.01
Green's Gluten Free Dubbel	Belgium	Gluten Free Dubbel	A dark gluten free beer - smooth and sweet.	7%	Low	17 oz Bottle	$9.01
Estrella Damm Daura	Spain	Gluten Free Pale Lager	Less then 6ppm	5%	Low	11 oz Bottle	$5.40
Ipswich Brewing Celia	VT	Gluten Free Saison	An actually GOOD gluten free beer!	7%	Low	12 oz Bottle	$5.40
Omission Widmer Pale Ale	OR	Gluten Free	Brewed like any other beer / enzyme removes gluten	6%	33	12 oz Bottle	$4.50
Element Plasma	MA	Gluten Free	Brown rice, malted millet, malted buckwheat & hops	9%	Low	25 oz Bottle	$19.81
Farnum Hill Dooryard	NH	Hard Apple Cider	Dooryard is basically the apple blend of the day	7%	N/A	25 oz Bottle	$18.20
Citizen Cider The Dirty Mayor	VT	Hard Apple Cider	Brewed with Ginger	7%	N/A	16 oz Bottle	$9.10
Stowe Cider	VT	Hard Apple Cider	Experience idyllic Vermont with Stowe cider	7%	N/A	22 oz Bottle	$11.71

West Brattleboro Pizza

1012 Western Avenue
West Brattleboro
Normal Pick-Up Time: 15 Minutes

HOURS
Daily 10:30 AM - 10 PM
CALL BEFORE LEAVING HOME!

802-257-0008

Name: _____

Phone #: _____

LG 18"	MED 14"	PIZZA	SM 10"
12.75	10.00	Cheese	7.00
14.25	12.00	Pepperoni	7.75
14.25	12.00	Mushroom	7.75
14.25	12.00	Onion	7.75
14.25	12.00	Green Peppers	7.75
14.25	12.00	Hamburg	7.75
14.25	12.00	Sausage	7.75
14.25	12.00	Bacon	7.75
14.25	12.00	Canadian Bacon	7.75
14.25	12.00	Sliced Ham	7.75
14.25	12.00	Eggplant	7.75
14.25	12.00	Chicken	7.75
14.25	12.00	Plum Tomato	7.75
14.25	12.00	Spinach	7.75
14.25	12.00	Pineapple	7.75
14.25	12.00	Broccoli	7.75
14.25	12.00	Garlic	7.75
14.25	12.00	Black Olive	7.75
14.25	12.00	Feta Cheese	7.75
15.75	13.00	Grilled Chicken	8.25
15.00	12.50	Comb. of Two	8.00
15.75	13.00	Comb. of Three	8.25
16.75	13.50	Comb. of Four	9.00
19.75	15.00	Special	9.25
15.00	12.50	Hawaiian	8.00

LG 18" SPECIALTY PIZZA   19.75
Verona *(Basil, Tomato, Garlic & Romano)*
Buffalo Chicken *(Chicken & Hot Sauce)*
Grizzly *(Pepperoni, Hamburg, Sausage, Ham & Bacon)*
Veggie (Tomato, Mushrooms, Spinach, Onions, & Green Peppers)
Ranch (Bacon, Tomato, Ranch Dressing, Mozzarella & Provolone)
Mediterranean *(Tomato, Black Olive, Spinach, Feta & Garlic)*

CALZONE *Topped w/garlic butter and our cheese blend*
1 Topping	9.00
2 Topping	9.50

APPETIZERS
Buffalo Wings *(10 pieces)*		6.75
Mozzarella Sticks (8)		6.75
Jalapeno Popper		7.25
Onion Rings		6.50
Garlic Bread w/ Cheese	3.75	4.75
Chicken Fingers & Fries		6.75
French Fries		4.00

SWEETS		DRINKS	
Carrot Cake	3.50	20 oz.	1.75
NY Cheesecake	3.50	2 Ltr	2.75
Baklava	3.00	Beer	3.75
		Fountain	1.45

GRINDERS	LG	SM
Chicken Parm.	6.50	5.75
Eggplant	6.50	5.75
Meat Ball	6.50	5.75
Veal Parm.	6.50	5.75
Sausage	6.50	5.75
Pepperoni	6.50	5.75
Genoa Salami	6.50	5.75
Ham	6.50	5.75
Italian	6.50	5.75
Roast Beef	6.50	5.75
Turkey	6.50	5.75
Pastrami	7.00	
Steak	7.00	6.50
Tuna	6.50	5.75
Veggie	6.50	5.75 -
BLT	6.50	5.75
Gyro	7.00	
Grilled Chicken Gyro	7.00	
Cheeseburg	6.50	5.75
Grilled Chicken Breast	7.00	6.00
WRAPS/ PITA	7.00	

SPAGHETTI	*Served with garlic bread*
Meat Sauce	7.00
Meat Balls	7.50
Sausage	7.50
Mushrooms	7.50
Eggplant	7.50
Chicken Parm.	7.50
Veal Parm.	7.50

DINNERS	*Served with garlic bread*
Lasagna	8.25
Veggie Lasagna	8.25
4 Piece Chicken Dinner w/ Fries	7.95

Burgers	*Deluxe comes with Fries*
Hamburger Deluxe	6.95
Cheeseburger Deluxe	7.00
Double Cheesburger	7.50
Bacon Cheeseburger	7.25

SEAFOOD	
Clam Basket	7.50
Fish 'n Chips	7.50
Scallops	7.50

SALAD	
Anti-Pasto	7.25
Greek Salad	6.25
Garden	6.00
Tuna	6.75
Turkey	6.75
Grilled Chicken Salad	7.25

STAY   **GO**   **PAID**

Add 10% meals tax

North American Restaurants on the Web

Restaurants in One American Community

http://www.whetstonestation.com/

http://www.vermontmarina.com/

http://www.thenewenglandhouse.com/

http://kringlefarmtable.com/

http://fireworksrestaurant.net/brattleboro/

http://www.3stonesrestaurant.com/

http://www.pandanorth.com/

http://www.topofthehillgrill.com/

http://www.thegleanery.com/

http://jdmcclimentspub.com/

http://curtisbbqvt.com/

http://www.putneyvillagepizza.com/

http://tcsrestaurant.com/

http://www.anchorseafoodrestaurant.com/

Restaurant Chains
around North America
(a sample from
http://www.restaurantchainlinks.net)

http://www.applebees.com/

http://aubonpain.com/

http://www.batonrouge.ca/

http://www.benjerry.com/

http://www.benihana.com/

http://www.bertuccis.com/

http://www.bostonpizza.com/ (BP)

http://www.cactusclubcafe.com/

http://www.caferio.com/

http://www.thecheesecakefactory.com/

http://www.chezcora.com/

http://www.chart-house.com/

http://www.chipotle.com

http://www.copelandsofneworleans.com/

http://dallasbbq.com/

http://www.durangosteakhouse.com/

http://www.elephantbar.com/

http://www.harveys.ca/

http://www.ihop.com/

http://www.kelseys.ca

http://www.legalseafoods.com/

http://www.mccormickandschmicks.com/

http://www.montanas.ca/

http://www.mrmikes.ca/

http://www.olivegarden.com/home

http://www.pfchangs.com

http://www.redlobster.com/

http://www.swisschalet.com/

http://www.tgifridays.com/

http://www.timhortons.com/ca

http://www.unos.com/

http://wolfgangpuck.com/

Answers

1 Breakfast

I. Match

1 – I	6 – D
2 – E	7 – B
3 – H	8 – J
4 – F	9 – G
5 – C	10 – A

II. Fill in each blank with a form of the key word and a pronoun.

1 – sweeten . . it
2 – scramble . . them
3 – boil . . them
4 – fry . . them
5 – slice . . it
6 – beat . . them
7 – chop . . it
8 – spread . . it
9 – poach . . them
10 – grind . . it
11 – prepare . . it
12 – mix . . it

III. Fill in

1 – prepared . . chopping
2 – sweeten
3 – Poached . . boiling
4 – Scrambled . . frying
5 – prepared . . mixing, beating, . . mixture
6 – spread
7 – sliced
8 – grind
9 – fried . . scrambled . . poached/boiled
10 – prepare

IV. Fill in

prepared . . slice . . spread , , grind . . sweeten . . mixture . . chopped . . mixed/scrambled . . sliced . . mixture . . spread . . sliced . . sweeten

2 Cereals, Breads, and Pastries

I. Match

1 – D	7 – H
2 – L	8 – B
3 – C	9 – K
4 – G	10 – F
5 – J	11 – E
6 – A	12 – I

II. Fill in

1 – process
2 – flake
3 – coat
4 – split
5 – nutrition
6 – baked
7 – snack
8 – ingredients
9 – crisp
10 – crunchy
11 – fortify
12 – Powdered

III. Fill in

1 – flakes . . flakes
2 – ingredient
3 – coated
4 – baking
5 – snack
6 – process
7 – forts/fortifications
8 – nutrition
9 – crispness . . crunchy
10 – split
11 – Powder . . powder

IV. Fill in

flakes . . powder . . coated . . nutritious . . crisp . . crunched . . baked . . ingredients . . processed . . crunchy . . splitting . . snack . . fortified

3 Breakfast + Lunch = Brunch

I. Match

1 – E	7 – F
2 – G	8 – K
3 – H	9 – L
4 – I	10 – C
5 – B	11 – A
6 – J	12 – D

II. Fill in

1 – alcohol
2 – stir
3 – occasionally
4 – Smoking/curing . . preserving
5 – fancy
6 – squeeze . . brew
7 – sweet tooth
8 – appetizer
9 – socialize

III. Fill in

1 – stirrer
2 – smoked
3 – fancy
4 – Brewed
5 – sweet tooth
6 – squeeze
7 – appetizer
8 – socializing
9 – occasion
10 – alcohol
11 – preserve
12 – cure

IV. Fill in

socializing . . fancy . . smoked . . cured . . alcoholic . . stirrers . . preservatives . . brewing . . squeezing . . sweet . . occasion . . appetizer

4 Lunch

I. Match

1 – E	7 – J
2 – F	8 – A
3 – G	9 – K
4 – H	10 – I
5 – C	11 – B
6 – D	

II. Fill in

1 – grilled
2 – toasted
3 – thick
4 – Sip
5 – chunks
6 – Stews
7 – spoons
8 – chips . . pickle
9 – kosher
10 – spoiled
11 – melted

III. Fill in

1 – stew
2 – sip
3 – chips
4 – grilled
5 – kosher
6 – thickens
7 – chunks
8 – toast
9 – spoon
10 – spoiled
11 – melted
12 – pickle

IV. Fill in

kosher . . grilled . . toasted . . melted . . sipped . . spooned . . thickened . . stew . . pickle . . chip . . chunked . . spoil

5 The Lunch Box and Brown Bag

I. Match

1 – H	7 – D
2 – K	8 – B
3 – J	9 – E
4 – C	10 – G
5 – I	11 – F
6 – A	

II. Fill in

1 – packed
2 – contains
3 – skin
4 – crumbs
5 – wrapped
6 – Fresh . . canned
7 – shell
8 – moistness . . stale
9 – core
10 – thermos

III. Fill in

1 – container . . pack
2 – wrap . . wrapping/
    wrapper
3 – can . . canned
4 – shell . . pack . . shell
5 – core . . core . . cored
6 – moistness . . fresh
7 – crumbs . . core
8 – Stale . . skin

IV. Fill in

pack . . wrap . . egg . .
chip . . fresh . . fresh . .
wrap . . stale . . shell . .
moistness . . fresh . .
can . . cores . . skins . .
crumbs

6 Pizza

I. Match

1 – F	7 – J
2 – H	8 – B
3 – L	9 – I
4 – A	10 – E
5 – G	11 – C
6 – K	12 – D

II. Fill in

1 – milder
2 – delivery
3 – ordered
4 – dishes
5 – toppings
6 – crumble
7 – grate
8 – server
9 – tastes
10 – Dough
11 – oven
12 – crust

III. Fill in

1 – crust
2 – deliver
3 – toppings
4 – order
5 – server
6 – oven
7 – Dish
8 – taste
9 – mild
10 – crumbled
11 – grated
12 – Dough

IV. Fill in

A – cheese . . toppings
B – mild . . dough
A – crust
B – dish
A – taste
B – crumble
A – oven
B – order
A – delivery service

7 Comfort Food

I. Match

1 – D	7 – A
2 – J	8 – B
3 – K	9 – F
4 – H	10 – E
5 – I	11 – G
6 – C	

II. Fill in

1 – pudding
2 – flavoring
3 – starch . .
       carbohydrates
4 – casserole . . noodle
5 – canned
6 – leftovers
7 – vegetarian
8 – masher
9 – sauce . . potholder

III. Fill in

1 – Vegetarians
2 – can
3 – mash
4 – Carbohydrates
5 – Noodles
6 – pudding(s)
7 – sauce
8 – leftovers
9 – flavors
10 – Casseroles
11 – starch
12 – potholders

IV. Fill in

noodle . . casserole . .
sauce . . mashed . .
pudding . . flavoring . .
carbohydrates . . starch . .
vegetarian . . leftovers . .
can . . potholders

8 Dinner

I. Match

1 – F	7 – E
2 – G	8 – I
3 – L	9 – A
4 – J	10 – C
5 – K	11 – D
6 – B	12 – H

II. Fill in

1 – well-done
2 – rare
3 – medium . . rare
4 – doggy bag
5 – dressing
6 – supper
7 – peel
8 – decaf
9 – deep fry
10 – courses, . . entrée . .
     dessert

III. Fill in

1 – well-done
2 – medium
3 – rare
4 – supper
5 – course . . entrée . .
     dessert
6 – doggy bag
7 – dressing
8 – deep fried
9 – peel

IV. Fill in

baked . . dressing . .
dessert . . supper . .
course . . entrée . .
deep fried . . well-done . .
rare . . rare . . medium . .
doggy bag

Answers

9 Seafood Dinner

I. Match

1 – E	7 – L
2 – G	8 – C
3 – B	9 – A
4 – H	10 – J
5 – D	11 – F
6 – K	12 – I

II. Fill in

1 – freezer
2 – batter
3 – crack
4 – raw
5 – bony
6 – fillet
7 – staple
8 – shellfish
9 – seafood
10 – raised
11 – frozen; fresh caught

III. Fill in

1 – bones
2 – staple
3 – crack
4 – (fresh) caught
5 – Seafoods
6 – shellfish
7 – batter
8 – raw
9 – freezer
10 – raises
11 – frozen
12 – fillet

IV. Fill in

Seafood . . staple . .
shellfish . . fresh-caught . .
cracked . . batter . .
freezer . . farm . .
frozen . . raw . . shell . .
bones . . fillet

10 Thanksgiving

I. Match

1 – D	7 – C
2 – K	8 – J
3 – L	9 – B
4 – A	10 – G
5 – E	11 – I
6 – H	12 – F

II. Fill in

1 – carving
2 – grace
3 – feast
4 – Cultivation
5 – Domesticated
6 – minced
7 – baste
8 – stuffing . . roasting
9 – harvest
10 – ladle . . creamed

III. Fill in

1 – grace
2 – baste
3 – ladle
4 – stuffing
5 – roasted
6 – domesticated
7 – cream
8 – cultivation
9 – minced
10 – carving
11 – feast
12 – harvest

IV. Fill in

feast . . harvest . .
domesticated . .
cultivated . . minced . .
grace . . roasting . .
basting . . stuffing . .
carved . . ladled . .
creamed

11 Cookouts

I. Match

1 – E	7 – L
2 – F	8 – A
3 – H	9 – C
4 – K	10 – D
5 – B	11 – J
6 – G	12 – I

II. Fill in

1 – dip
2 – whipping
3 – clambake
4 – charcoal
5 – tailgate
6 – crush
7 – vendor
8 – pit
9 – grill
10 – spit
11 – skewer
12 – barbecue

III. Fill in

1 – clambake . . tailgating
2 – dip
3 – whipped
4 – crushed
5 – vendor
6 – charcoal
7 – grill
8 – pit . . pit
9 – spit
10 – barbecue
11 – skewers

IV. Fill in

clambake . . pit . . dip . .
vendors . . spit . .
tailgate . . skewers . .
grilled . . barbecue . .
charcoal grill . .
crushed . . whipped

12 Picnics

I. Match

1 – D	7 – A
2 – F	8 – C
3 – L	9 – G
4 – H	10 – I
5 – K	11 – E
6 – J	12 – B

II. Fill in

1 – alfresco
2 – jug
3 – cooler
4 – tablecloth
5 – picnic basket
6 – dehydrated
7 – garbage . . compost
8 – napkins
9 – soft drinks
10 – blanket
11 – camp stove

III. Fill in

1 – soft drinks
2 – jug
3 – napkins
4 – camp stove
5 – compost . . garbage
6 – dehydrated
7 – cooler
8 – blanket
9 – tablecloth
10 – alfresco
11 – basket

IV. Fill in

blanket . . blanket . .
tablecloth . . cooler . . soft
drinks . . jug . .
camp stove . . basket . .
napkins . . garbage . .
compost . . dehydrated
alfresco

13 Fast Food

I. Match

1 – E	7 – C
2 – G	8 – A
3 – B	9 – F
4 – I	10 – D
5 – J	11 – K
6 – H	

II. Fill in

1 – steamed
2 – greasy
3 – straw
4 – lid
5 – condiments
6 – recycled
7 – disposable
8 – wrap
9 – ready-made
10 – deli
11 – food cart
12 – unappetizing

III. Fill in

1 – Straw
2 – greasy
3 – ready-made
4 – lids
5 – wrap . . food cart
6 – steam
7 – Disposable
8 – condiments
9 – deli
10 – unappetizing
11 – recycled

IV. Fill in

Deli
unappetizing
ready-made
wraps
kosher
condiments
greasy
straws
condiments
recycle
disposable

14 Coffee Shops

I. Match

1 – E	7 – J
2 – D	8 – B
3 – H	9 – C
4 – K	10 – F
5 – I	11 – A
6 – G	

II. Fill in

1 – aroma
2 – barista
3 – pastry
4 – gourmet
5 – regular
6 – mug
7 – coffee beans
8 – atmosphere
9 – caffeine
10 – dark roast . . stimulant
11 – grind

III. Fill in

1 – atmosphere
2 – pastry
3 – coffee beans
4 – gourmet
5 – caffeine
6 – aroma
7 – barista
8 – mugs
9 – grounds
10 – regular
11 – stimulant
12 – dark roast

IV. Fill in

mug . . dark roast . .
caffeine . . barista . .
pastry . . atmosphere . .
stimulates . . gourmet . .
aroma . . beans . .
grounds . . regular

15 International Restaurants

I. Match

1 – G	7 – A
2 – I	8 – D
3 – C	9 – H
4 – B	10 – J
5 – K	11 – F
6 – L	12 – E

II. Fill in

1 – silverware
2 – customers
3 – special
4 – spicy
5 – familiar
6 – take-out
7 – ethnic
8 – reservations
9 – inviting
10 – informal
11 – chopsticks
12 – exotic

III. Fill in

1 – exotic
2 – reservations
3 – silverware
4 – familiar
5 – invitation . . informal
6 – customer
7 – chopsticks
8 – spicy
9 – special
10 – ethnic
11 – take-out

IV. Fill in

ethnic . . familiar . .
spicy . . chopsticks . .
silverware . . customers . .
take-out . . specials . .
exotic . . inviting . .
informal . . reservations

16 The Brewpub

I. Match

1 – H	7 – L
2 – D	8 – B
3 – F	9 – C
4 – J	10 – A
5 – I	11 – K
6 – E	12 – G

II. Fill in

1 – bartender
2 – foam
3 – on tap
4 – sports bar
5 – booth
6 – kegs
7 – tasteless
8 – weak
9 – draft . . Brewery
10 – head
11 – regulars

III. Fill in

1 – bartender
2 – head
3 – booth
4 – tasteless
5 – brewery
6 – sports bar
7 – keg
8 – weak
9 – regulars
10 – on tap . . draft
11 – foam

IV. Fill in

regulars . . Sports Bar . .
bartender . . kegs . .
head . . foam . .
tasteless . . Brewery . .
draft . . booth . .
tasteless . . on draft

Lesson 13: page 49   *Lesson 14: page 53*   *Lesson 15: page 57*   *Lesson 16: page 61*

Answers

17 Supermarkets

I. Match

1 – G	7 – A
2 – J	8 – K
3 – I	9 – C
4 – B	10 – F
5 – H	11 – E
6 – D	

II. Fill in

1 – cashier
2 – scanned
3 – checkout
4 – goods
5 – salad bar
6 – department/ aisle
7 – Prepared food
8 – reusable
9 – produce
10 – aisle
11 – Dairy
12 – barcode

III. Fill in

1 – prepared foods
2 – salad bar
3 – department
4 – produce . . scanned . . barcode
5 – dairy
6 – goods
7 – reusable
8 – checkout
9 – cashiers
10 – aisle

IV. Fill in

department . . check-out . . cashier . . scanned . . . barcode . . produce . . aisle . . reusable . . goods . . froze . . f rozen . . dairy . . salad bar . . prepared foods

18 Convenience Stores, Coops, and Farmers' Markets

I. Match

1 – F	7 – D
2 – H	8 – A
3 – I	9 – E
4 – B	10 – C
5 – J	11 – G
6 – L	12 – K

II. Fill in

1 – locavore
2 – certified
3 – groceries
4 – beverages
5 – growers
6 – pickers
7 – season
8 – stocked
9 – supplies
10 – local
11 – Free-range
12 – organic

III. Fill in

1 – growers . . seasonal . . pickers
2 – supplier . . beverages
3 – groceries . . stocking
4 – locavore
5 – free-range . . organic
6 – certifies
7 – local

IV. Fill in

organic . . free-range . . local . . groceries . . beverage . . stocking . . season . . picked . . local . . suppliers . . growers . . locavore

19 The Kitchen

I. Match

1 – G	7 – A
2 – H	8 – J
3 – D	9 – E
4 – B	10 – I
5 – K	11 – C
6 – F	

II. Fill in

1 – bowl
2 – equipment
3 – knife
4 – recipe
5 – paring
6 – teaspoon
7 – measuring
8 – cut up
9 – spatula
10 – gadget
11 – appliance
12 – tablespoon

III. Fill in

1 – knife
2 – appliances
3 – gadget
4 – bowl
5 – equipment
6 – cut . . up
7 – recipe
8 – paring knife
9 – spatula
10 – Tablespoons . . teaspoons
11 – measure

IV. Fill in

teaspoon . . knives . . paring . . spatula . . measuring . . bowl . . recipe . . cut up . . gadgets . . appliances . . equipment

20 Health and Food

I. Match

1 – I	7 – G
2 – H	8 – E
3 – C	9 – K
4 – J	10 – B
5 – A	11 – F
6 – L	12 – D

II. Fill in

1 – anorexic
2 – obese
3 – portions
4 – caloric
5 – junk food
6 – diet
7 – nutritious
8 – allergic
9 – diabetes
10 – gluten
11 – label
12 – intolerance

III. Fill in

1 – junk food
2 – calories
3 – label
4 – intolerant
5 – allergies
6 – obese . . diabetes
7 – gluten
8 – anorexic
9 – portions
10 – nutritious
11 – diet

IV. Fill in

diet . . obesity . . anorexia . . calories . . portions . . allergies . . junk food . . label . . intolerant . .diabetes . . gluten

Lesson 17: page 65   *Lesson 18: page 69*   *Lesson 19: page 73*   *Lesson 20: page 77*

21 Vegetarianism

I. Match

1 – F	7 – E
2 – D	8 – A
3 – H	9 – C
4 – K	10 – I
5 – J	11 – B
6 – G	

II. Fill in

1 – contain
2 – stock
3 – poultry
4 – pasta
5 – tofu
6 – grains
7 – greens
8 – vegan
9 – avoid
10 – vitamins
11 – raw . . alternative

III. Fill in

1 – poultry
2 – contain
3 – alternative
4 – green
5 – raw
6 – vitamin
7 – vegan
8 – Tofu
9 – pasta
10 – grains
11 – avoid
12 – stock

IV. Fill in

veganism . . alternative . .
avoid . . stock . . poultry . .
greens . . grains . . tofu . .
pasta . . contain . .
vitamins . . raw

22 Cooking

I. Match

1 – D/I	7 – L
2 – G	8 – C
3 – I	9 – H
4 – K	10 – B
5 – A	11 – J
6 – F	12 – E

II. Fill in

1 – Evaporation
2 – flames
3 – sauté
4 – sear
5 – simmer
6 – stove
7 – device
8 – burners
9 – coil
10 – thermometer
11 – broiler
12 – rack

III. Fill in

1 – oven
2 – temperature
3 – device
4 – burner
5 – sauté
6 – flames
7 – simmer
8 – coil
9 – sear
10 – Evaporated
11 – stove . . racks

IV. Fill in

1 – racks
2 – simmer
3 – evaporated
4 – sear
5 – Sauté
6 – flame
7 – coiled
8 – burner
9 – stove
10 – broiling
11 – Thermometer
12 – device

23 Recipes

I. Match

1 – D	6 – A
2 – F	7 – C
3 – G	8 – H
4 – I	9 – E
5 – B	

II . Fill in

1 – quarts
2 – liquid
3 – dry
4 – thermometer
5 – step . . rinse
6 – thaw
7 – pan
8 – pot
9 – flour
10 – pint
11 – cup

III. Fill in

1 – quart . . pint
2 – cup
3 – liquid
4 – dried
5 – scale
6 – pot . . pan
7 – thawed
8 – rinsed
9 – steps
10 – Flour

IV. Fill in

scale
1 – Step . . dried
2 – thaw
3 – rinse
4 – pan
5 – cups
6 – quart . . pot
7 – flour . . liquid
8 – boiling
9 – Add . . stir
10 – Simmer . . stirring . .
    pints

Lesson 21: page 81   *Lesson 22: page 85*   *Lesson 23: page 89*

❦ 125

Food Names Index The numbers are lesson numbers.

ale 16
apple 5, 10, 12
apple cider 12
artichoke 6
arugula 8
asparagus 21

back bacon 24
bacon 1, 22
bagel 2
baloney 5
banana 5
basil 6, 15
bass 9
beans 1, 7
beef 4, 7, 21, 23
beefsteak 24
beer 6, 8, 11, 12, 16
beignet 24
berries 8
biscotti 14
blueberry 24
Boston baked
 beans 24
bread 2, 10, 13, 20, 21
bread crumbs 23
broccoli 10
brown sugar 7
bun 6, 13
burger 16
butter 1, 7, 14, 17, 21, 23

candy 18
carrot 4, 19, 23
catfish 9
celery 3, 23
cereal 2

challah 3
cheddar cheese 24
cheese 1, 7, 12, 13,
 17, 21, 23
chicken 5, 7, 8, 11,
 18, 21
chili 15
chili con carne 24
chips 12
chocolate 13
chocolate chip 5
chop 8
chowder 4
cinnamon 2
clam 4, 9, 11
cloudberry 24
coffee 1, 8, 18
cookie 5
corn 2, 7
cornbread 24
corn chips 18
corn cob 3
corned beef hash 3
corn on the cob 11
Cornish pasty 24
crab 9
cracker 4
cranberry 10
crawfish 24
cream 2, 11, 14
cream cheese 2
creamer 1
crepe 24
croissant 2, 14

dairy products 20, 21
dessert 6

donut 2, 14

egg 1, 7, 9, 17, 20, 21
eggs Benedict 3
energy drink 1
entrée 8
espresso 14

fat 2
fish 9
fish and chips 13
flounder 9
flour 2, 9, 18, 23
focaccia 6
French fries 13
French toast 3
fried chicken 13
fries 16
fruit 1, 8, 10, 18, 21

garlic bread 15
goat cheese 6
grain 2
granola, 2
grapefruit 3
green pepper 8, 11
grits 1
guacamole 16
gumbo 24

ham 1, 7
hamburger 11, 13, 22
hard-boiled eggs 12
hash browns 1
herb 6
hollandaise sauce 3
home fries 8

honey 2, 17
hot chocolate 1, 14
hot dish 24
hot dog 11, 13
huevos rancheros 3

ice cream 11
iced tea 11

jam 1, 14 , 17
jambalaya 24
jelly 1
juice 1, 10

ketchup 13
kidney 10
king crab 24

lamb 7, 8, 21
lasagna 7
latte 14
lemon 3, 19
lemonade 12
lettuce 4, 8, 13, 17, 23
liqueur 8
liver 10
lobster 9, 11
lobster roll 24
lox 3

macaroni 7
maple syrup 3, 17
mayonnaise 4
meatloaf 7
meats 11, 18, 21, 23
milk 2, 7, 9, 10, 13,
 17, 18

milkshake 13
molasses 7
Montreal bagel 24
mozzarella 6
muffin 2, 14
mushroom 1, 7, 8
mustard 7, 13

nachos 11
Navajo fry bread 24
noodles 20
nut 2, 8, 20

oatmeal 2
oats 2
octopus 9
okra 24
olive oil 6, 8, 23
omelet 1
onion 1, 7, 8, 10, 11,
   13, 23
orange 3, 19
oyster 4, 9

pancakes 3
Parmesan 6
pasta 7
pastry 2
peanut butter 5
peas 4, 7, 10, 21, 22

pemmican 24
pepper 12, 13
pepperoni 6
pickles 12
pie 6
pineapple 6
poi 24
pork 1, 7, 8, 21
potato 1, 7, 8,
   10, 19, 21, 23
potato chips 11, 18
potato salad 13
poultry 8
poutine 24
pumpkin 10

radish 8
raisin 2, 10
red snapper 9
relish 13
rib 8
rice 2, 7, 21
roast beef 8
roast chicken 18
roll 4, 13
rosemary 6

salad 4, 21
salmon 9
salsa 11

salt 12, 20, 23
sausage 1, 13
scallops 9
scone 2, 14
seafood 11
shell 1
shish kebab 11
shortening 2
shrimp 9
soft drink 6
soul food 24
soup 18
soybeans 21
spaghetti 7
Spam 24
spice 15
spinach 23
sprouts 8
squash 10, 21
squid 9
steak 8, 10, 21
stout 16
strawberry 13
strawberry
   shortcake 11
sucre á la
   crème 24
sugar 1, 7, 14
sushi 18
sweet roll 2

taro 24
tea 14
tilapia 9
toast 1
tomato 3, 8, 13
topping 6
tripe 24
trout 9
tuna (fish) 4, 7, 9
turkey 5, 8, 21, 23
turnip 24

vanilla 13
vegetable 1, 10, 11,
   17, 18, 19, 21, 22, 23
venison 10
vinegar 4, 8
vitamin 2
vodka 3

waffles 3
walleye 24
wheat 2, 21
wine 6
wings 16

yogurt 5
yolk 1
Yorkshire pudding 24

Key Word Index The numbers are lesson numbers.

aisle 17
alcoholic 3
alfresco 12
allergic 20
alternative 21
anorexia 20
appetizer 3
appliance 19
aroma 14
atmosphere 14
avoid 21

bake 2
barbecue 11
barcode 17
barista 14
bartender 16
baste 10
batter 9
beat 1
beverages 18
blanket 12
boil 1
bone 9
booth 16
bowl 19
brew 3
brewery 16
broil 22
burner 22

caffeine 14
calorie 20
camp stove 12
can 5
canned 7
carbohydrate 7
carve 10
cashier 17
casserole 7
charcoal 11
checkout 17
chip 4
chop 1
chopsticks 15

chunk 4
clambake 11
coat 2
coil 22
compost 12
condiments 13
contain 21
container 5
cooler 12
core 5
course 8
crack 9
creamed 10
crisp 2
crumb 5
crumble 6
crunchy 2
crushed 11
crust 6
cultivation 10
cup 23
cure 3
customer 15
cut up 19

dairy products 17
dark roast 14
decaf 8
deep fried 8
dehydrated 12
deli 13
deliver 6
department 17
dessert 8
device 22
diabetes 20
diet 20
dip 11
dish 6
disposable 13
doggy bag 8
domestic 10
dough 6
draft 16

dressing 8
dry 23

entrée 8
equipment 19
ethnic 15
evaporate 22
exotic 15

familiar 15
fancy 3
farm raised 9
feast 10
fillet 9
flake 2
flame 22
flavor 7
foam 16
food cart 12
fortify 2
free-range 16
freezer 9
fresh 5
fresh-caught 9
frozen 9
fry 1

gadget 19
garbage 12
gluten 20
goods 17
gourmet 14
grace 10
grains 21
granular 2
grated 6
greasy 13
greens 21
grill 4, 11
grind 1
groceries 18
ground (coffee) 14
grower 18
harvest 10

head 16

(in)formal 15
ingredient 2
intolerant 20
inviting 15

jug 12
junk food 20

keg 16
knife 19
kosher 4

label 20
ladle 10
leftover 7
lid 13
liquid 23
local 18
locavore 18

mashed 7
measure 19
medium 8
melt 4
mild 6
mince 10
mix 1
moist 5
mug 14

napkin 12
noodle 7
nutritious 20

obese 20
occasion 3
on tap 16
order 6
organic 18
oven 6

pack 5
pan 23
paring knife 19
pasta 21
pastry 14

peel 8
pickle 4
picnic basket 12
pint 23
poach 1
portion 20
pot 23
potholder 7
poultry 21
powder 2
prepare 1
prepared foods 17
preserve 3
processed 2
pudding 7

quart 23

rack 22
rare 8
raw 9
raw food 21
ready-made 13
recipe 19
recycle 13
regular (coffee) 14

regulars 16
reservation 15
reusable 17
rinse 23
roast 10

sauce 7
sauté 22
scale 23
scan 17
scramble 1
seafood 9
sear 22
serve 8
shell 5
shellfish 9
silverware 15
simmer 22
sip 4
skewer 11
skin 5
slice 1
smoked 3
snack 2
socialize 3
soft drink 12

spatula 19
special 15
spicy 15
spit 11
split 2
spoil 4
spoon 4
sports bar 16
spread 1
squeezed 3
stale 5
staple 9
starch 7
steamed 13
step 23
stew 4
stimulant 14
stir 3
to stock 18
stock 21
stove 22
straw 13
stuffing 10
supper 8
supplies 18
sweeten 1
sweet tooth 3

tablecloth 12
tablespoon 19
tailgate 11
take-out 15
taste 6
tasteless 16
teaspoon 19
thaw 23
thermometer 22
thermos 5
thick 4
tofu 21
topping 6

unappetizing 13

vegan 21
vegetarian 7
vendor 11
vitamin 21

weak 16
well-done 8
whipped 11
to wrap 5
a wrap 13

Other Books from Pro Lingua on Reading and Vocabulary

Lexicarry. A vocabulary builder that features over 2500 captionless pictures. An English word list is in the back of the book, and word lists in ten other languages are available as booklets or free on the web. The illustrations are grouped into Communicative Functions, Sequences, Related Actions, Operations, Topics, Places, and Proverbs and Sayings. All levels.

Getting a Fix on Vocabulary. This is a student text with CD that focuses on word building through affixation – prefixes and suffixes – and learning common Latin and Greek roots. The vocabulary is presented in the context of newspaper articles and radio news broadcasts, and practiced in a variety of exercises. Intermediate–Advanced.

A to Z Picture Activities: Phonics and Vocabulary for Emerging Readers. The book is divided into units, one for each letter of the alphabet. The units all start with a worksheet page of phonics featuring the sounds that letter can make with sample useful words that make those sounds. All are amusingly illustrated in a style as appropriate for adults as for children. Each unit also contains pages of illustrated vocabulary on specific topics, such as **A**nimals, the **B**ody, **C**olors, **D**ays, **E**ating, etc.

Go Fish. A collection of 86 pairs of brightly colored vocabulary cards showing pictures of the rooms of a house (kitchen, livingroom, etc.) and things you would find in a home. In addition to the Go Fish game, six other games are explained. Suitable for beginners.

The Learner's Lexicon. A list of 2400 words arranged in four levels; 300 (limited survival), 600 (surviving), 1200 (adjusting), and 2400 (participating). A reference for teachers developing their own lessons and curricula.

American Holidays. Twenty readings and exercises that follow the same format as *Potluck*. Includes all the national holidays, special days (Valentines, etc.), and religious holidays. CD available. Intermediate.

Coloring in English. A coloring book/vocabulary builder for beginners of all ages. Dozens of high-frequency nouns as sight words.

Got It! A game for building vocabulary and conversation skills. Groups compete to compile lists of words that relate to a topic. 40 topics; 160 possible games. All levels.

Lessons on Life, Learning, and Leadership. Short readings for developing critical thinking skills. Includes cultural notes and lexical challenges. High intermediate-Advanced.

Read and Learn. In this low-level series, there are four colorful graded readers with high-interest articles of 50, 75, 100, and 125 words. Brief vocabulary, reading, and grammar exercises enhance each article. CDs available. Beginner to Low intermediate.

For information or to order, please visit **ProLinguaAsssociates.com**